## Praise for *Do You Love Football?!*

"Gruden has written a page-t[...]
*ball?!*] offers some interestin[...]
youngest coach to win a Supe[...]
most colorful and charismat[...]
storytelling is a strength."

"[*Do You Love Football?!*] provides valuable insight into the life of a football coach. . . . Written with humility and humor, which may surprise readers, given Gruden's fierce on-field visage."
—*Dayton Daily News*

"A fast-paced, intense, and sometimes wisecracking memoir. . . . The effect is similar to sitting in a sports bar swapping stories with Gruden. . . . [He] serves up slices of himself, sprinkled with humor and heavily laced with football philosophy. . . . A fun, lighthearted look at what makes Gruden tick."
—*Tampa Tribune*

"Gruden gleans wisdom from the colorful likes of Bobby Knight, Bill Walsh, and other legendary coaches with whom he has worked. Players, too, are sketched vividly and personally. . . . It's Gruden's own portrait that emerges most sharply: he's the scrappy private who almost imperceptibly becomes field commander. . . . He's also funny and self-deprecating. . . . The point of it all is that football isn't about winning but about learning how to win."
—*Publishers Weekly*

"Just another book by a football coach about winning and hard work? Hardly. . . . Gruden takes us with him on a romp through his past. . . . [He] has lived life like he coaches: there's no sense being there if you don't give it your all."
—*Booklist*

"Gruden fans will eat up this candid, entertaining memoir."
—*Dallas Morning News*

# Winning with Heart, Passion, and Not Much Sleep

# Do You Love Football?!

## Jon Gruden

### with
## Vic Carucci

Perennial

*An Imprint of* HarperCollins*Publishers*

First Perennial edition published 2004.

Designed by Elliott Beard

Library of Congress Cataloging-in-Publication Data is available.

ISBN 0-06-057945-5

04 05 06 07 08 ❖/RRD 10 9 8 7 6 5 4 3 2 1

To Mom, for helping me find my passion. To Dad, for showing me the way. To Cindy, for making tremendous sacrifices as a wife and mother that allow me to do this job. To Deuce, Michael, and Jayson, for constantly reminding me of what is truly important in life. To Jay and Jim, for providing all of the inspiration and support that a brother could ever want. To all of the coaches and players it has been my great privilege to work with and compete against, and to all of those coaches and players out there I haven't met yet. I know you love football!

—J.G.

To Rhonda, Kristen, and Lindsay. I know this is another dedication, for another book, but you are a one-of-a-kind family. I can't tell you enough how much I love you and how blessed I am to have you in my life.

—V.C.

# CONTENTS

# Do You Love Football?!

# ONE

# "Do You Love Football?"

Well, do you? You love football? You do, don't you?
You love it! You know you love it!
—DAVE ADOLPH,
*linebackers coach, Oakland Raiders*

Loving every minute of the game-day experience.
(Tom Wagner/Tampa Bay Buccaneers)

As far back as I can remember, I've lived and died on every game day. I don't think I can ever recall a time when football—in one form or another—didn't have a major influence on everything I thought, everything I said, everything I did.

High school. College. Pro. Our family was moving around with each coaching job my dad held at all three levels. Or I was playing quarterback in high school. Or I was hoping to see the field as a college quarterback. Or I was changing coaching jobs myself in a never-ending quest for knowledge and improvement.

Football really is all I know. Other than going to the beach once in a while and watching the waves, it's really the only interest I have outside of my wife and our three boys. I'm not a scratch golfer. I don't know how to bowl. I can't read the stock market. Hell, I have a hard time remembering my wife's cell phone number. But I can call, "Flip Right Double X Jet 36 Counter Naked Waggle at 7 X Quarter" in my sleep.

I love the competition of the game. I love the players who play it. I love the strategy, the variables. I love the smell of the grass, the sound of the stadium. I love the thrill of victory. I like to see how we respond to the adversity that a loss brings and to the sudden changes that we have to deal with, whether it's a fumble, an interception, a fifteen-yard penalty, or something worse, like our right tackle suffering a broken ankle. What's the weather going to be like? What kind of crowd will we have?

Football is the ultimate team game. There are just so many people who play a role. There are trainers, managers, coaches, players, fans, media. It's just so exciting. I consider myself fortunate to have been able to see it at such close range for so long.

The game day experience is what really gets me juiced. I'm up at 3:17 A.M. most days, and that includes the morning of a game. Home or away, we stay at a hotel the night before, and I'm always waiting for the newspaper guy to make his delivery to my room at five-thirty. At breakfast I'm waiting for the eggs to come out, even though I don't eat very much. If we're on the road I'm waiting for the first bus to the stadium to arrive at the hotel (for home games I usually catch a ride with Bill Muir, our offensive coordinator and line coach).

Once I'm at the stadium I sit at my locker and for the next three, four or five hours before kickoff I go over my sideline sheet, which contains the offensive game plan, minus the diagrams. We probably carry about 125 passes and maybe 30 runs into each game, but the typeface on the sideline sheet has been reduced small enough so that they all fit on both sides of an eight-and-a-half-by-eighteen-inch piece of paper that I laminate and can refer to while I'm calling the plays from the sideline.

I have columns for different situations—first-and-ten, first-and-fifteen, second-and-one-to-five, second-and-six-to-nine, second-and-ten-plus, third-and-short (one to three yards), third-and-medium (four to six yards), third-and-long (seven to ten yards), third-and-extra (beyond ten yards)—and the calls I can make in each of them. I have columns for different spots on the field, such as the "red zone," which I break down into plus-five, plus-ten, plus-fifteen and plus-twenty, with five or ten runs and passes in each. I have columns for goal line, short yardage, play passes, nickel passes, nickel runs, nickel blitzes, Cover Nine (our term for two-deep zone). I might even have a Keyshawn Johnson column, and at some point I'll look down at it and say, "I've got to get him involved. I've got to get him going." Okay, okay, I've got to get him the *damn* ball.

I prioritize the calls that I've gone over with the staff and the quarterbacks the night before the game, but when I get to the stadium I say to myself, *Okay, what if I use number one? What if I use number two? Do I really like number three? What if they start playing a lot of Cover Nine? Do I have enough Cover Nine throws in the game plan?* I'll make notes to myself on the sideline sheet, which also has the first names and numbers of each of the officials (just in case I have any reason to have a nice chat with them during the game) and the names of three of the most important people in my life—my sons, Deuce, Michael and Jayson. I'm usually feeling pretty guilty late in the week when I'm at the office working on the game plan instead of being home with those guys and my wife, Cindy. Seeing their names helps me to maintain a little sense of balance when I need it the most, such as in the middle of a game when the running battle between your head and your heart can easily tilt you too much in one direction or another.

I take different colored Sharpie fine-point pens—red, blue, green and black—and use certain colors to highlight sections of the sideline sheet and to write notes. Using these colors is the only thing I'm superstitious about. I'll say, "Ah, the green pen's in a slump; I'm getting it out of here. I'm using black and red this week." If we kick somebody's ass, if we play a really good game, I'll say, "I'm going to stay with red for the next couple of games. Red's hot." It's silly, I know, but you don't want to mess with the mojo.

The sideline sheet is everything to me. We have our first fifteen plays scripted—as most teams have been doing ever since Bill Walsh, the godfather of offensive football, had so much success doing it—because you always want to have that beginning point for your offense. You need that preview of exactly how you intend to attack your opponent, but I also love to think about situations that are going to come up along the way. I just know Derrick Brooks is going to scoop a fumble or he's going to intercept a pass or he's going to do both. We are going to generate turnovers, and when we get a sudden change in our favor, the crowd's going crazy, the offense is running out there and we're first-and-ten at midfield. What do you call? When Brian Kelly intercepts a pass and runs it down to the two-yard line, what do you call? Do you go right to your goal-line column or do you go to your plus-five passes?

The sideline sheet represents a week of hard work. I like knowing that we have a heck of a plan, that we've worked it all week and that on top of that we have contingency plans that are well thought out before the game so that we don't have to make eighteen different adjustments at halftime. We have Plan C if Plan B goes awry. If Plan C doesn't work, Plan D isn't a bad way to go, either. And if Plan E is necessary, by God, I've got that, too. The sideline sheet is my crutch, my all-in-one tool, my security blanket.

After I'm done reviewing the sideline sheet, I greet the players as they come in the locker room. Quite often I will ask guys the same question that I pose practically every day of the week: "Do you love football?"

By week ten, week eleven, these guys start to get the long eyes and it becomes tough to get them up for practice on Wednesday and Thursday. So when I spot one of them in the hall, instead of just saying hello or nodding my head, I'll get kind of a crazy look on my face and ask, "Do you like football? Do you? Do you love football? Do you love it? You do, don't you? You love football, don't you? I know you love football."

It's my way of reminding them that the only reason you're playing football or coaching football is because you have a love for it, and that passion is a powerful force that can carry you through any obstacle that gets in your way. Don't get totally bent out of shape with what the writers are saying or what the pressures of the game bring. We're playing and coaching because we love the game, man. How the hell else can you explain putting on shoulder pads and cranking into a Crowther blocking sled or diving for a catch and landing on the ground twice a day during the hottest month of the year in training camp? How the hell else do you work like we work as players and coaches unless you love it?

The origin of my "Do you love football?" question goes back to 1998, after the very first game of my very first season as a head coach. My debut with the Oakland Raiders, on *Sunday Night Football*, was ugly. U-G-L-Y. Kansas City kicked our asses 28–8 in Arrowhead. Sacked us ten times. Made for one of the longest and most humiliating nights of my life. We flew back to Oakland that night, landing at about four in the morning. I slept on the floor of our facility, as did the rest of the coaches. I woke up a few hours later and got a cup of coffee. As I sat in my office, feeling like a total moron at 0–1, Dave Adolph, our linebackers coach, walked in. It was pretty obvious I was in need of some sort of morale boost. I think Dave, who was about sixty years old at the time and had seen a whole lot more football than I had, was checking to make sure that I wasn't packing my stuff and getting ready to head out the door for good.

"You like football?" he said in a loud, raspy voice, knowing full well that at that point I was hating football, myself and the day I signed that first contract to become a head coach. I looked at Dave and smiled, probably for the first time since we had boarded our flight to Kansas City two days earlier.

"Well, do you?" Dave asked again. "You love football? You do, don't you? You love it! You know you love it!"

I nodded. Dave was absolutely right. I loved the game enough to understand that as horrible as I felt, I was ready to come back for more, ready to put it all on the line the following week against our next opponent. As ugly as that game had been, I was going to experience others that were just as ugly, if not uglier. But I will keep coming back for more—every day, every practice, every game, every season—until I don't have a team to coach.

Another favorite part of my pregame routine is going out to see the stadium, just to get a feel for the environment we're going to play in. I walk around the field, check out the stands. I'm just taking it all in with my eyes, my ears, my nose. Little by little, step by step, I get myself worked up into the excitement of game day.

There's nothing like going into a locker room after a big win, or walking off the field after winning on the road—after taking one from *their* fans and *their* friends and *their* families—and then getting on a plane and enjoying a three-hour flight home. All of a sudden you don't mind feeling sore and tired. There's validation, there's justification, there's worth. The investment paid off. Winning and enjoying it with others are the two greatest feelings in this business. You work your butt off all year, around the clock, to try to find a way to beat this team on this day, regardless of what time the game is or where it is.

To help a player succeed is different from being the player on the field having the success, but it's certainly just as satisfying. I know because I've been on both ends of it. I know how hard it is to play this game because I wasn't a very good player myself. Probably the most disappointing thing in my life is that I never amounted to anything but a ham-and-eggs backup quarterback for a Division III college. But there's tremendous satisfaction from being involved in determining the structure of practice, in putting together the game plan, in picking the right plays to call and, finally, in the outcome of it all. I look at my role as a coach the same way I look at being a teacher, like my mother was, helping a student to get an A. The student got the A, but he needed the teacher's help to get it.

Sometimes losing teaches you a lot more about yourself and your team than you ever learn from winning. It's easy to be a winner. It's easy to react positively when things go well. Normally, when you lose it's because "You didn't throw the ball to this guy enough . . . This guy wasn't involved enough . . . We had too many injuries." In other words, there are just too many excuses, too many ways to shift blame. Which is natural, because after all we're human and there are emotions in this business that you have to deal with. But that's when you've got to rely on leaders. You've got to rely on the head coach, assistant coaches and key players to help you through that time. It isn't easy. Believe me, it isn't easy.

But you will battle through it. Sometimes you'll start the year off with a heartbreaking overtime loss—and five months later have it end in the Super Bowl. That's how it went for the Tampa Bay Buccaneers last season, my first as their head coach. There I was on September 8, 2002, in Raymond James Stadium watching a botched punt in OT become an intercepted pass in our end zone to hand the New Orleans Saints a 26–20 victory in my official debut with the Buccaneers. And there I was on January 26, 2003, standing on a platform in the middle of Qualcomm Stadium in San Diego, celebrating our 48–21 victory over the Raiders in Super Bowl XXXVII.

It's hard to believe that such a range of emotions can be separated by such a relatively short amount of time. But, you know, it's also hard to believe a lot of the things that happened to me in the course of the year and in the course of my career. One minute someone's calling you in the middle of the night telling you that you've been traded—yes, traded—from Oakland to Tampa Bay. The next minute you're trying to sell yourself and your ideas to players and coaches whose love and loyalties still belong to the man you're replacing. The next minute you're in the Super Bowl . . . staring across the field at guys you coached and coached with for four years.

As exciting as it was to be up on that platform, I will never forget the feeling of being on the sideline before kickoff. Right behind me were Paul Warfield, Larry Csonka, Don Shula, Bob Griese, Nick Buoniconti, Larry Little, and Jim Langer. These Hall-of-Famers from the 1972 Miami Dolphins, the only undefeated team in NFL history, were there to participate in the pregame coin toss. These are men who became immortal when they beat the Washington Redskins in Super Bowl VII and finished that season 17–0. And when they saw me, they said, "Hey, Coach Gruden, good luck to you." All I could think was *Holy Toledo! They know who I am. A little ham-and-egger from the University of Dayton is talking to Don Shula and Paul Warfield and Larry Csonka.*

Right there it began to hit me how far I had come on this wild and wildly fast journey. At thirty-nine I knew I still had plenty of miles to go. I knew that there was still a whole lot more for me to learn and accomplish. To that point, though, I realized how much I had benefited from being around brilliant front-office people and some exceptional coaches. I've always considered the experience the football version of an Ivy League education, like graduating from Harvard, only with pigskin instead of sheepskin. And no one could have had a better live-in professor than my own dad, Jim Gruden, who has helped and encouraged me every step of the way.

As the Dolphin Hall-of-Famers walked out for the coin toss I got on the headset to my younger brother, Jay, who worked as an offensive assistant on our coaching staff during the season, and said, "You should see Larry Csonka, man. I'll bet he was a bitch to tackle." Jay laughed. Pretty goofy stuff to be talking about only minutes before the biggest game of our lives, don't you think? But that's what football is all about—plugging into the energy and excitement of the moment, reflecting on the memorable games and plays of the past, pondering the many challenges ahead. There really is nothing like it.

You can always find something to complain about in life. I've never liked being around a guy who has a litany of excuses, a guy who bitches all the time. In other words, the kind of guy I was on the way to becoming earlier in my career. It took my dad to set me straight. We always talk by phone four or five times a week. After getting off to a 1–3 start in my first year as offensive coordinator of the Philadelphia Eagles, I was bitching to my dad about everything.

"Man, we're just terrible," I said. "We can't do anything right. We're going to get our asses kicked."

I was looking for a little sympathy, maybe a little understanding from someone who would know exactly where I was coming from and, as a bonus, might just hate to hear one of his boys sounding so unhappy. Did I ever have the wrong person for that.

"Hey, if you don't like it, why don't you leave?" my dad said. "If you don't like it, then get the hell out of town. Do something else, because this is coaching football.

"You've got a great opportunity, son. You're the offensive coordinator of the Philadelphia Eagles. Do it! Coordinate the offense!"

I got off the phone and realized that he was absolutely right. You can go through this business complaining about everything. Even though we wound up winning the Super Bowl, there were a lot of reasons for me to bitch and make excuses during last season: Oh, man, I have to put together a new coaching staff because all the assistants I had in Oakland were under contract. Damn, we've lost Marcus Jones, one of our defensive ends, for the whole year with a knee injury. Geez, we haven't had Anthony McFarland, one of our starting defensive tackles, for almost half of the regular season because of his broken forearm and broken foot, and now we won't have him for the playoffs. Golly, Brad Johnson, our starting quarterback, is going to miss the last two games of the season with an injured back.

I don't want to be like that. I don't want anybody around me to be like that. We're here for a very short time, and we're in the NFL. Are you kidding me? What an ideal setting to have some fun. If you don't have fun coaching or playing in the NFL, where are you going to have fun in America? You travel on a beautiful jet airplane. You stay in a Ritz-Carlton. You eat the nicest food you could ever think of eating. You have a police escort to the stadium. You have brand-new footballs. You have socks that fit and stay up perfectly. You have a stadium packed with fans.

It's exciting as hell.

Now, it's not easy. There are all kinds of challenges to face, all kinds of reasons to whine. But nobody wants to be around a whiner. Nobody wants to hear your excuses. Does that mean I'm always fun to be around? Get real. To be honest, there are a lot of times when I can be a miserable sonofabitch. I've been accused of being a guy who sometimes has to be miserable to be happy. I don't know why that is. What I do know is that I don't ever want to get the feeling that everything's perfect, everything's rosy because that's when you lose your edge. If you let that happen to you, you're dead.

Peek into my brain and you'll see what I mean. On any given day, I'll be thinking things like:

*You won a big game, so what? We've got to play these guys now. They're bigger and stronger than the team we saw last week.*

*How come our third-round draft pick from last year is not performing up to the standards that we expected him to?*

*Hey, what's the deal with this weight machine? How come the Denver Broncos have a bigger one than ours?*

*Oh, you won the Super Bowl. That's great. But we haven't won a game this year, have we? What are we going to do this year?*

I'm still in search of what I call the Master Game Plan, the head coach/offensive coordinator's Holy Grail. That's the one where your opening possession's a nine-play, eighty-yard touchdown drive. You never punt. You never turn the ball over. You never commit a penalty. You score touchdowns on every series. You score seventy, eighty points in a game. That's what we're after. It can be done. It will be done in the NFL. If I can't aim high, aim for the absolute best, aim for what some people might think is impossible, well, if I can't do that, what's the use?

I also know this: Through the highest of highs and the lowest of lows, you're always going to be ahead of the game if you love what you do for a living. It's like Kathy Gruden taught her three sons while we were growing up: "The most important thing is to find your passion and go after it."

For me and for Jay, it's football. Hell, Jay's thirty-six years old and he's still playing quarterback for the Orlando Predators of the Arena Football League. For my older brother, Jim, it's an entirely different calling; he's a successful radiologist. You can bet that Jim is every bit as passionate about that as his two brothers and our father are about football, and as our mother was throughout her teaching career.

You only live once, so you might as well find something that you love to do and do it. Get after it. Max out.

# TWO

# Doing It the Knight Way

"We are not going to tolerate error!"
—COACH BOBBY KNIGHT

A young football dreamer.
(Courtesy of the author)

**M**Y DAD'S INVOLVEMENT in football sparked my love for the game and my desire to pursue a career in coaching. He's still involved, as a consultant to our player personnel department, which he joined in the summer following his retirement after sixteen seasons as a regional scout for the San Francisco 49ers.

How about that? I've got my dad providing his scouting expertise. I've got my brother Jay helping me call plays from the press box. All I have to do now is hire Jim as one of our team doctors and we'll have the Gruden family pretty well covered.

Before I was even born my dad was assistant football coach at Fremont Ross High School, located about twenty miles outside of Sandusky, Ohio. That was where I joined the Gruden roster, but it wouldn't be long before football would cause my dad to make a series of moves throughout the state—to Crawford, where he was head coach at Galion High; to Tiffin, for an assistant coaching position at his alma mater, Heidelberg College, where he had also played quarterback; to another assistant's job at the University of Dayton, where John McVay was the head coach at the time before going on to coach the New York Giants and become general manager of the 49ers.

Wayne Fontes, former coach of the Detroit Lions, and his brother, Lenny, who was an NFL assistant, were also on that Dayton staff. Lenny had a son by the same name. Whenever the Flyers played at old Baujan Field, young Lenny and I would pick up about nine or ten of those red paper Coke cups off the ground, crumple them up and jam them together until we formed the shape of a football so we could play our own little game of tackle in the end zone as the actual game was going on. That is, until someone would run us out of there.

In 1973 my dad made his first big jump when he became running backs coach for Lee Corso at Indiana University. I was ten years old when he took the job, and I remember every one of those players. While my dad and I were sitting in field-level seats at one of my brother's arena football games, my dad suddenly pointed to the guy holding the down-and-distance marker on the sidelines.

"That's Dale Keneipp," he said.

"Number thirty-seven?" I said.

My dad almost fell out of his chair because I had remembered Dale's number and the fact he had played safety for Indiana in 1973.

Not long after that I got a call from my dad, who told me that Walter Booth, a cornerback on that '73 Indiana team who went on to become a lawyer, wanted to talk to me about investing some of my money.

"Number six?" I said.

I can remember Trent Smock and Keith Calvin at receiver, Scott Arnett at quarterback, Mike Harkrader at tailback, Courtney Snyder at halfback and Rick Enis at fullback. I can name the whole team, even though the way it performed on the field could make a lot of those guys easy to forget. Our best season was 5–6. We got our brains beat in by the Big Ten powerhouses like Ohio State and Michigan.

While living in Bloomington, Indiana, I became friends with Tim Knight, a fellow member of the Working Men's 49ers Pop Warner football team. He was just like me, the son of a coach. The only difference was his father was Bobby Knight. I don't give a damn what sport we're talking about, he sets the standard for coaches everywhere. Coach Knight would take the IU basketball team all over Indiana, to places like New Castle and

Fort Wayne, just to play scrimmages. There is no way to overstate Indiana's obsession with basketball. The movie *Hoosiers* has it exactly right. Sometimes Tim would call up and invite me to come along as one of the ball boys with him, and that made me one of the luckiest kids in the world. I'd be riding on a bus, throughout the state of Indiana, with the IU basketball team. I'll never forget it. Tim and I would sit in the back, eating grape candy with Quinn Buckner, Bobby Wilkerson, Wayne Radford and Kent Benson.

Once we went into the locker room at halftime, and Knight wasn't only coaching his starters; he was coaching the whole team. I stood there quietly and was just blown away. I remember him talking about defense. Well, not talking—screaming. Yelling about playing defense and hustling. Giving a thorough demonstration of the difference between a stationary and a moving pick. I also remember that his players gave him their full attention when he walked in that room—and tremendous respect. It was clear to me then that Coach Knight is a true leader and puts his whole being into what he does.

There was a lot of conformity there, which was something my dad understood better than I did at the time. He told me that I had to have my hair cut before I got on the basketball team's bus. I was pissed about that because I thought I looked kind of cool with the long, scraggily hair I had back then. But the rules were the same for every kid with any connection to the IU team: no earrings, no jewelry, no tattoos and, unfortunately, hair above the ears. When we would stop at a restaurant for dinner on the way home, everyone was reminded about table manners and proper conduct. Assistant coaches were on top of every detail. It was a class operation. It was about how to become a man.

Coach Knight's practices were like games. Actually, they were harder than games. Honest to God, his practices were longer than and as intense as anything I had ever seen. They were physical. They seemed to last forever. It was not "Go out there and shoot ten free throws." It was "Go out there and *make* ten free throws." It was structured to be very situational and as gamelike as possible. The biggest points that Coach Knight would stress were "Don't make stupid mistakes! Don't get careless with the ball! Take high-percentage shots! Fundamentals! Techniques! We are not going to tolerate error! We are not going to tolerate undisciplined, careless error! We are not going to have that at Indiana! It . . . is . . . not . . . going . . . to . . . happen!"

Those were the words that you heard all the time. And I do mean all the time. He established a sense of urgency to get it right in practice. When you laced them up for Knight at Indiana or you lace them up for him now at Texas Tech, whatever time practice starts, you'd better be there five minutes early. You'd better be mentally prepared to execute—which means you'd better have studied your game plan the night before—because it's going to be mentally as well as physically taxing. If you're a star player, if you're Kent Benson or Quinn Buckner, you're going to get coached just as hard as Tom Abernethy and Jim Crews.

While basketball's not football—maybe we've got a lot more situations to practice because there are eleven guys on the field and a football field's a lot bigger than a basketball court—the lessons I learned from being around the Indiana basketball team are still with me. The most valuable: Teach your players how to practice. That's even more important than teaching them what to practice, because if you don't establish the pace you want and if you aren't consistent about it, they're going to work the way they want to and it's going to change with each day. You have to let them know that you want them practicing hard, with a sense of purpose, every time. With us, there are no thirty-five- to forty-minute breaks where we're just walking around and playing grab-ass. This is dress rehearsal, man. Our performances are live.

There's absolutely a correlation between practicing well and playing well. Players can see the film, why they're doing what they're doing, but at the same time if they half-ass their way through a day of practice, they're not going to have a true feel for what it's going to be like on game day. You want them walking off that field and going to bed at night knowing they've had a really good week of practice and are prepared to play. It builds confidence that everyone—players and coaches—will carry into the game. That is the Bobby Knight way.

Even though I was only in eighth grade, I got to attend Coach Knight's basketball camp for high school players. There must have been about two thousand kids packing the IU dorms. Coach Knight never showed up the first two days. When he finally walked in to address us for the first time, it got really quiet. We were holding our breath, waiting to hear what he was going to say. In typical Bobby Knight fashion, he didn't start off with one of those mushy, phony-sounding "Welcome to my camp, kids . . . we're going to have a great time" lines. He started off by asking questions.

"How many of you guys play high school basketball?"

Everybody raised his hand.

"How many of you guys don't like your coach?"

About forty guys raised their hands.

"What makes you think your coach likes you?"

That, right there, was a big lesson that I have always carried with me. I didn't take a survey, but it's a pretty safe guess that most of the guys who indicated they didn't like their coach felt that way because they weren't starting; backup players always think they should be starting unless they happen to be one of those rare individuals who is just happy to be on the team. Maybe they thought their coach made them work too hard or was too demanding. Coach Knight's point was that the relationship between a player and a coach is a two-way street and that a coach, either professionally or personally, just might not like a particular player. You always read about the player saying he's unhappy with his coach, but do you ever stop and consider that his coach might not be too fond of him, either?

When I was third-string quarterback at Dayton, it would have been so easy for me to talk about not liking my coach. It would have been so easy to bitch about working so hard in practice, yet never really getting the chance to prove that I should be the starter. Then I'd think back to what Coach Knight said and I'd begin to see that maybe the coach just didn't like me because I wasn't playing well or because maybe, in his eyes, I just wasn't working hard enough to become better. There can be a lot of reasons. Sometimes a coach dislikes a player to the point where he eventually becomes an ex-player. My dad taught me long ago that if you're not a smart guy, if you're not really instinctive and you make a lot of mistakes, you're not going to play. I'd hear him talk about a guy who had a hard time picking up the offense or who had a hard time executing properly, and what he'd usually say was, "Man, I don't like that player . . . Man, this guy kills me."

As a coach, it's hard to genuinely like or love all the guys on your team. You've got to respect them. You've got to coach them. You've got to work together, but when you think you can please everybody all the time and make everybody like you all the time, you're living in la-la land. We've got to be professional and we've got to have a common goal, which is to win. But we don't have to go to the beach together and go to dinner together and like the same movies and read the same books and listen to the same music. That's why Baskin-Robbins has thirty-one different flavors of ice cream.

I know that Coach Knight has done some things that are controversial, and he has to answer some questions. But I love that guy. He has always been great to my family and me. When my mom had a cancerous kidney taken out many years after we left Bloomington, I don't know how he found out where she was, but he sent her a huge, beautiful painting of the IU basketball uniform—jersey, shorts, Adidas high-tops and socks—with a personal, handwritten note.

Every time I pick up the newspaper, I look to see how Coach Knight's Texas Tech team is doing. He still looks like he did in '73 at Indiana and his teams still win. If I could be like that thirty years down the road, I'd count myself the luckiest man alive.

# THREE

# Notre Dame, Dan Devine, and the Best and Worst of Witnessing Greatness from the Inside

Showing my Fighting Irish pride with Mom and brother Jay.
(Courtesy of the author)

**W**HERE IT ALL REALLY KICKED IN for me, where football became a part of my very soul, was in 1978, when the late Dan Devine hired my dad to be the running backs and special teams coach for the Fighting Irish of Notre Dame. You had that enthusiasm—that genuine enthusiasm—around the program. You had the class and mystique of the Irish. You had the pride of the gold helmet. You had the special kind of kids who go to Notre Dame. Those were the guys I wanted to be like: Joe Montana, Blair Kiel, Vegas Ferguson.

All highlighted by that unbelievable fight song: "*Cheer, cheer for old Notre Dame . . .*" Hell, I still get the goose bumps whenever I hear it or whenever I see the Fighting Irish on television.

I began playing quarterback as a freshman at South Bend Clay High School. Dad would actually bring Notre Dame players to my football games. Seeing those guys in the stands jumping up and down, watching me play . . . man, I was in my glory.

When my dad was coaching at Indiana I had followed the Hoosiers' football team as religiously and as adamantly as I followed Notre Dame. But we took some real head-kickings at Indiana. Now we were on the other end of that. Instead of seeing my dad sitting at the kitchen table on Saturday night with his head down, not even touching his meal, he's going out to dinner and having alumni smacking him on the back.

And you have that fight song. And you have that national ranking in the newspaper. And you have everyone wondering, *Who are we going to drill this week?* That was awesome, man.

I was involved with the football team in every way they would let me be involved. Dan Devine had no problem allowing the coaches' sons to hang around the team. Normally it all depends on the head coach's policy. Some head coaches don't want kids around. Some head coaches couldn't care less, and that was Dan. When I wasn't at school I was down at the ACC, the Athletic Convocation Center on Notre Dame's campus. I would go in and lift weights with all the football players. I was part of the team's strength-and-conditioning program. I was watching spring practice. I knew all the players and they knew me. They were my heroes, my idols. The longer I was around the team and the older I got, the more involved I became with it, because I was closer in age to the players. Blair Kiel, our quarterback, would leave his car at our house because his mom and dad wouldn't let him have it on campus. So, never one to pass up a good opportunity, I would drive Blair's Pontiac Firebird out on dates.

All my dad's running backs would come over to the house. Jimmy Stone, who wore forty-two; Phil Carter, twenty-two; Greg Bell, twenty-eight; Vegas Ferguson, thirty-two; Larry Moriarty, thirty-seven; Pete Buchanan, thirty-five. No, I did not have to look up any of those numbers. I know them by heart. And some things they did are hard to forget. Greg Bell once ripped the rim right off our backboard. He was supposedly the Ohio dunk champion, which, considering that he stood barely six-foot, I found hard to believe. I even told him, "You're too short to dunk it." So he jumped up and ripped down our backboard. End of conversation.

My dad would bring home all sorts of Notre Dame football gear. I wore Notre Dame turf shoes to class. I wore green and gold sweat tops. I wore Vegas Ferguson's actual jersey to class; it would hang down to my knees.

We had AstroTurf in the basement of our house in South Bend. The wallpaper was a giant photograph of a crowd at a game. We had the yard markers and lines on the turf. We had replicas of the national championship banners up. We had the fighting leprechaun painted on our wall. It was a shrine to Notre Dame.

Of course, with all the time I spent with my dad at work, the actual campus was my home away from home. There were two reasons I shadowed him like that. One, it was fun to be around the ultimate college football environment. Two, it was usually the only way I could get to see my dad for any length of time because he wasn't home a whole lot. I was with him during practices. I listened to him call recruits on the phone. I'd go to basketball games and sit next to a kid whom he was recruiting for the football team, and watch him sell the kid. At some point my dad would always have to go see someone else or have some phone calls to make, so I'd end up sitting alone with the recruit. Afterward my dad would ask, "Hey, did so-and-so have a good time?"

"Yeah, Dad, he was really into the game. I think he's going to come to school here. He seemed fired up."

I was like his spy and would give my dad feedback on how all the visits went. One time I sat in the student section at a Notre Dame basketball game with Neil Maune, a top offensive lineman from Missouri. As usual, the students were on their feet from beginning to end—with one notable exception. When the game was over, I told my dad, "I don't think you're getting Neil Maune."

"Why?"

"The whole game, he never stood up. He just sat there reading something, not even watching the game. He acted totally uninterested."

To my dad's relief, Maune did end up signing with the Fighting Irish after all. It turned out that he just didn't like basketball.

I never accompanied my dad on the trips he made to recruits' homes, but I heard he was a great setup guy for the head coach to be the closer in the house. I realize it's easier to recruit football players for Notre Dame than for Indiana, especially at that time, but my dad was as relentless as hell. He covered all the bases. He was really good at finding out who was going to be the biggest influence on a recruit's decision—the high school coach, the kid's mom, his stepdad—and he would work on that person just as hard as he worked on the recruit.

I used to watch my dad coach his running backs; my brother Jay and I sometimes would be the quarterbacks for his ball drills. I didn't know the playbook and I wasn't aware of all the protections that were called and so forth, but I knew that my dad knew what he was talking about. I knew that he had his players' attention. I knew that every year he was there, Notre Dame had a thousand-yard rusher.

It also was no coincidence that the backs my dad coached hardly ever turned the ball over. He demanded excellence. He set a standard that his players had to follow and they followed it—or they didn't play for him. What came through loud and clear from my dad was that you should try not to have guys on your team who repeatedly make mistakes and if you do, try to replace them as soon as possible.

I'd love to tell you about how I witnessed one of the greatest moments in the history of Notre Dame football—the 1979 Cotton Bowl against Houston. But I can't. That's because I only stuck around long enough to see us fall behind 34–12. New Year's Day, 1979, brought one the worst ice storms in the history of Texas. It was cold, windy, miserable as could be. A lot of people left the game early. Unfortunately I picked that game as the first and only time I had ever walked out on the Fighting Irish while my dad was on their coaching staff.

I was with my best friend, Scott Johnson. His father is Jim Johnson, the outstanding defensive coordinator of the Philadelphia Eagles. Jim worked with my dad on that Irish staff and at

Indiana before that. Anyway, as painful as it still is to admit, Scott and I walked out on Notre Dame, got on one of the team buses, and just waited to go home—with our heads in our hands. Then some frostbitten lady got on the bus. She had sucked it up and stayed the whole game. "That's the greatest game I've ever seen," she said through chattering teeth. "We won!"

At first we thought she was smoking something. We went running down to the locker room, slipping and sliding the whole way. When we got there, I couldn't believe my eyes. My dad was on the floor, celebrating with the players. As soon as he spotted me, he jumped up and grabbed my shoulders.

"Did you see the end of that game?" he yelled.

I almost didn't have the heart to answer him, but I knew I had to.

"Uh, no," I said in a faint voice.

"He missed the whole thing," said my brother Jay, who had toughed it out and was all too happy to inform our father about what a wimp I had been. "He was on the bus."

On the bus and unaware of the incredible magic that Joe Montana was performing inside the stadium. The last I knew he had been sick. He had missed most of the third quarter because of a below-normal body temperature. By the time he returned, the game looked pretty much out of hand. And with Joe sick and us trailing by twenty-two points, the ice storm provided a good excuse for Scott and me to leave. Who could have ever imagined that Joe would be able to fight off his illness and rally us to a 34–34 tie on the final play of the game? Who could have ever believed that it would come down to Joe Unis, a Dallas native, kicking the extra point with no time remaining to give the Fighting Irish a 35–34 victory.

Even worse than missing Montana's heroics was not seeing two of the guys who we were hanging around with all week—Steve Cichy and Tony Belden, B-team players who were just getting their first taste of action—play a huge role in the win on special teams. Steve blocked a punt and Tony caught it and ran it in for a touchdown to give us a chance near the end. Those were the guys playing pinball with us during the week.

My dad still busts my chops about leaving that game early. When we're playing golf and he's three shots up on me after three holes—as is usually the case because he's an excellent golfer—he says, "I'll bet you want to go get on the bus and leave, don't you? I know you want to get on the bus."

I was there only for Joe Montana's senior year so I didn't get to know him really well. Of course, I'm not so sure how close we would have been even if I had lived in South Bend through his entire college career. He was Joe Cool, the first genuine superstar player that I had ever been around, and I was too intimidated to even approach him.

When I went to work for the 49ers as an offensive assistant in 1990, I think he remembered me as that little skinny guy who was always staring at him like some weirdo. I was as intimidated by him at San Francisco as I was at South Bend, but there were a lot of assistant coaches and head coaches and front-office people that were also intimidated by Joe along the way, for sure.

Joe was special. He had that charisma about him like no one else I had ever been around. He was the Pied Piper. Everybody loved him, and he had an unbelievable following from everywhere. How he lasted until the third round, I'll never know. He must have had some bad workouts before the draft.

But Joe was an iceman. What he did at Notre Dame, bringing teams from behind, was absolutely amazing. Forget about the '79 Cotton Bowl. What about the '78 game against USC in the LA Coliseum? I can still remember it as if it were yesterday. We were getting our brains kicked in and Joe brought us back by leading us on three fourth-quarter touchdown drives to give us a 25–24 lead with a minute left. Then a bad call screwed us. After driving the Trojans to midfield, Paul McDonald got hit while dropping back to pass and fumbled. The officials ruled the pass incomplete, but to this day I know that that was a fumble. Anyhow, the clock stopped, McDonald completed a quick pass and that set up Frank Jordan's winning thirty-seven-yard field goal with two seconds left. I'm still pissed off about that game.

With Joe in there you just knew when we got the ball back, we were going to win the game because that guy was going to do whatever it took to make it happen. And, by God, he did.

I didn't really have a lot of drawn-out conversations with Dan Devine, except for one. We were playing Air Force and we were beating them 24–0. I was a junior in high school and a guy in his mid-forties sitting behind me was on the offense's ass—which meant he was on my dad's ass and on all the offensive coaches' asses—the whole game. And it was 24–0. And we were 9–0.

Finally I turned around and I said something mean to this guy. We got in a pushing-shoving contest and I just hauled off and cranked him. Smashed him right in his face. He went to hit me back and his metal watchband grazed the side of my face, tearing open my cheek. I had blood all over my face. Even though I got my shot in, it looked like I was the one who got drilled, like I was the one who got the big "L" in that bout. I was like Rocky Balboa. *Cut me, Mick!*

As the usher came to take me away, some of the coaches' wives were crying, probably because they saw me covered with blood but also because I think they were embarrassed by my behavior. Not long after that Coach Devine called me into his office. He made some fatherly points that, as a seventeen-year-old, I definitely needed to hear.

"Don't try and fight every individual battle, because you can't win every one," he said. "Choose your opponents carefully. This is Notre Dame and people expect a certain kind of conduct."

He challenged me to get some composure, but I know he

appreciated me sticking up for his coaches and for his team. My dad also was concerned about me and, in his own way, he, too, expressed his appreciation for my loyalty to the Fighting Irish and to him. He reinforced what Dan Devine said, telling me, "You've got to remain poised, keep your cool and walk away." I wasn't the biggest guy and I wasn't stupid. I was emotional, but I didn't go around the stadium during a game or the town or my school looking to pick a fight with anyone who ever said something bad about Notre Dame, the coaches in general or my dad in particular. Besides, I had a pretty sharp tongue myself, and that was how most of the altercations I was involved in were fought—in an exchange of words instead of an exchange of fists.

It's hard sometimes being a coach's son or being a quarterback's dad or being the wife of a player. Whenever a coach is fired or a player is traded or released, it's not just the player or coach who is involved. It affects a lot of other people—the family, the close friends. We lost to Clemson one year, and the next morning we found signs from moving companies, such as Allied Van Lines and United Van Lines, stuck in our yard. All the coaches had that done to them. Today, with talk radio and the Internet, with all the writing and chatting about every single thing that happens in sports, there's even more heat to take than there was then. There are a lot of people who live in the hometown of a team who you would expect to have a devoted relationship with that team, but it's not always the case.

I don't know if there are words to adequately describe my commitment to Notre Dame and its football program. I don't know if anyone could ever truly understand the depth of the love I had for the Fighting Irish.

And then one day it all disappeared.

That was the day my dad got fired by Gerry Faust, who took over as head coach at Notre Dame after the 1980 season. Although the team had finished 9–2–1 and played in the Sugar

Bowl—where we lost to Herschel Walker and the Georgia Bull-dogs—Dan Devine decided to retire because his wife had taken ill. Faust came from Cincinnati's Moeller High School, where in eighteen years he had a 174–17–2 record, including seven unbeaten seasons, five state championships and four mythical national prep titles.

As a result of the head coaching change, my dad and a few other assistants lost their jobs to make room for guys Faust wanted to bring in with him from Moeller and other places. Looking back on it now, I understand where Coach Devine was coming from. He was in his mid-fifties and had coached for more than thirty years. He was at a stage in his life where he had to do what he had to do. At the time, though, I was devastated. I didn't want to go down in the basement, where those Notre Dame banners were, anymore. I wanted to blow up our house.

I'm still, to some degree, bitter about my dad being let go by Notre Dame, because those were the three greatest years of my life. To have it all taken away was hard to get over. It was like I got fired, too. I lost my friends on the team. I lost my Notre Dame connections. I actually couldn't stomach the thought of them playing on Saturday without my being part of it. I felt betrayed.

That was my first close encounter with the harshest reality of the coaching business. I've since come to understand that getting fired is something all coaches go through if they're at it long enough. I understand now that it's a possibility no matter how good it's going. The Fighting Irish had been in the Sugar Bowl. My dad had recruited the number-one rated quarterback in each of three states (Chris Brown of Kentucky, Blair Kiel of Indiana and Scott Grooms of Ohio) and signed them all in same year. Do you know how hard that is to get three blue-chip kids at the same position, in the same class, to go to the same school? To do that with three guys is almost unheard of. And then you're fired?

Yes, I understand it happens that way sometimes, but it doesn't keep me from being mad as hell. That year I became one of those sour, angry hometown guys who was rooting against the Irish. I became the guy who was like the Grinch who stole Christmas. And when Faust decided to change the uniforms to those ugly royal blue jerseys, I hated Notre Dame even more. When the Fighting Irish went 5–6 in 1981, Gerry Faust's first year, that was the greatest year of my life. Those were the greatest eleven weeks of my life.

My experience at Notre Dame was one I wish every kid could experience. In fact, if you're an assistant on my coaching staff and you have a son and you want him to be a ball boy, then by all means bring him to practice. If you want to let him go in the meeting rooms and the locker rooms and the weight rooms, and he's old enough and can take care of himself, I'd love to have him come by. My three boys are a little too young for that, but I'd love to have the coaches' sons around. Why? Because I know what it's like to get to know the players and be a part of something special and the images that it left with me. I want to share that with other coaches' sons.

After being fired by Gerry Faust, my dad took a job out of football just so I could finish my senior year at South Bend Clay. He sold corrugated boxes for a year. And he was a hell of a box salesman. He made more money selling boxes than he ever made in coaching. He had a better car to drive. He had a bigger expense account. He got to see me play more. When he worked for Lee Corso for five years at Indiana, I never got to see my dad away from work, because he was almost never home.

At one point after his dismissal from Notre Dame, my dad started to talk about how guilty he felt because of all the time he had been away from us. He said he was giving serious thought to staying out of coaching for good so he could be around us more. I can relate to those feelings of guilt now, but back then I couldn't. "Are you nuts?" I told him. "You've got to get back into coaching." I'll admit my reasons for saying that were totally selfish. I loved having my dad around more, but I looked forward to game day too much for him not to go back to coaching. There's no game day in the box business.

Sure enough, once I graduated from high school my dad was right back in football, this time in the NFL as the running backs coach for the Buccaneers. My dad got knocked down, but he didn't stay down. He didn't even get his pants dirty. Instead of putting his energy into feeling sorry for himself, he put it into getting another job. That's a characteristic that I hope I have, that I hope we all have.

You've got to show resiliency. There are a lot of good coaches out there right now who are out of work. When it's my turn to join them, I hope I can rely on what I witnessed from my dad to push me through that time.

But as a coach, you can't be looking over your shoulder every second. People ask how difficult it is to be loyal to the club you work for, knowing full well that this is a business and that you could be out on your ass tomorrow. It isn't difficult at all, because you live in your hopes, not in your fears. If you're going to work every day waiting for the anvil to smash you right in the head, you're in the wrong business. You constantly work yourself into a fired-up, optimistic mentality, and you don't think about the consequences of losing. You don't think about getting fired. You don't think about all the negative things. Otherwise, you're going to be a basket case and not be able to coach anything.

# FOUR

# If You Can't Throw the Perfect Pass, Draw the Perfect Circle

The ham-and-eggs quarterback gets a rare glimpse
of the field. (John Moreau/University of Dayton)

SUPER BOWL XXXVII wasn't the first Super Bowl that I was in. I was the MVP of about sixteen or seventeen Super Bowls before that. At least in my mind I was.

When I was a kid I made every big play in every big game on the fields of my imagination. I'd stand in front of the mirror and pretend to be Curt Gowdy, telling millions of television viewers about what a sensational player Jon Gruden was. I loved Curt's voice. Sometimes I would be Dick Enberg saying, "Oh my!" as I threw touchdown passes, made diving catches, and went the distance on a handoff.

On Sundays in Dayton I'd be in front of the TV watching the Cleveland Browns in those white jerseys and white pants that would get all covered with mud. Then about midway through the first quarter I'd put on my number forty-four Leroy Kelly jersey, which my mother got for me by sending in a form on the back of a box of Aim toothpaste. I'd put on my plastic orange Browns helmet, and I'd be diving in the mud and running for touchdowns just like Leroy did. And like any hero-worshipping kid, I was always writing letters to that guy, telling him how great he was, asking for his autograph.

Bill Nelson was the Browns' quarterback at the time, and I was a pretty big fan of his as well. In 1982, when my dad went to coach for the Bucs, the quarterbacks coach was none other than Bill Nelson. "I can't believe it, Dad," I said, all excited.

"You're working with Bill Nelson." Apparently I didn't have a whole lot of company in that fan club because anyone else within earshot would say, "How in the hell do you know who Bill Nelson is?"

In the summer my dad would take me up to the Browns' training camp for a day to watch them practice, but we never got to any of their games. I followed basketball and baseball as well. I loved the Cincinnati Reds, the "Big Red Machine," and we did go to a lot of their games.

I pretty much had made up my mind about becoming a coach when I was fifteen, sixteen years old. Hell, as a teenager I practiced drawing circles just so that I could be good "on the board." That's a coaching term for drawing plays, illustrated with X's and O's, on the grease or chalkboard, which usually is the first test a young coach has to pass when he's interviewing for a job in any legitimate high school or college football program. I was always taught when they put you on the board, you don't want to look incompetent. You want to present yourself properly and professionally, which means being able to draw nice, round circles. Some people might think this is funny, but I'm serious when I say I'm one of the best there is at drawing perfect circles. I got that way by drawing hundreds of them, thousands of them.

When I wasn't following sports or dreaming about following my dad's footsteps into coaching, I was acing school, at least early on. I was a tremendous student in elementary school. I was a whiz when it came to spelling, addition, multiplication, and subtraction. I was always the last one left in spelling bees and the first to finish my times tables in math. All of that changed when I got to high school. My mind wandered a lot. I'd think of any number of things I wanted to do instead of my homework—like play Nerf basketball in my room or play Fotoelectric Football or watch a game on TV. I had no interest in geometry or algebra. I'd read a social studies book for an hour and wouldn't remember a word I read. Not one word.

My older brother, Jim, is a doctor. He's the director of cardio-thoracic imaging at Emory University's medical school and an adjunct professor of biomedical engineering at Georgia Tech. He was a 4.0 student. He was valedictorian at South Bend Clay and number one in his class at Notre Dame. He took the exit exam at the University of Miami Medical School and got the fifth-highest score in the history of the medical program there. He's a genius.

Then I come along and I'm getting a 2.0 and the teachers are calling my mom asking, "What's wrong with Jon?" There wasn't anything wrong with me. I struggled, but I wasn't dumb. Among the many things my mother understood quite well is that all kids, even siblings, are not the same. "Jon is different from Jim," she told my high school teachers. "He's doing the best he can. He's just not as good at algebra and geometry and social studies and chemistry."

Looking back, I probably could have applied myself more, but I hated those subjects. I hated every second I was in those classes. The only reason I liked going to some of them was maybe because I would be in there with a friend or a girl I liked. I just had to grit my teeth, suck it up and find a way to get through it. I really had no choice but to get through it. My dad gave me more than a few lectures in which he pointed out that if I were serious about pursuing a career in coaching, I needed to go to college. And if I wanted to go to college, I had to pick up my grades in high school.

"Get your act together, son," he told me.

I played every sport, but football was always my favorite. I was a five-nine, 175-pound high school quarterback who couldn't throw the ball very well and who wasn't very fast. But I threw for a fair amount of yards. In fact, not long after the Super Bowl somebody told me that one of my passing records at South Bend Clay was broken during the 2002 season. Another thing that got broken was my neck. It happened on a late hit I received as a junior. That put me out for the rest of the season, and for a while I had to wear one of those big collars. I hated that thing. Jay would look at me and say, "Nice neck." Maybe that explains why the collar would conveniently disappear whenever my parents weren't around and reappear when they were.

My favorite player at the time was Doug Flutie. We were about the same size and pretty close in age, so I wanted to be like him. I saw him doing his thing at Boston College and for a fleeting moment I thought maybe I, too, could play at Oklahoma or one of those bigger schools. When I started seeing these guys at Notre Dame—how big and how fast they were, how they threw the ball and how I threw it—it was pretty obvious I wasn't going to get a scholarship to any major college. Still, I loved to play. I figured I could land a spot on some small college team, and if nothing else I'd at least have a lot of fun.

I was worried about my SAT score, but much to my surprise I ended up with a 1030, which is pretty darn good, especially for someone like me and with no preparation. It's amazing what you can do when you're motivated. I knew I had to do well on the SAT—while also picking up my grades a little bit—just to get into college and keep that coaching dream alive.

I wanted to go to a school where I would have the best chance to play quarterback, and to play right away. I was recruited by Dayton and I had visited Dayton. My intention always was to go to Dayton, but I felt maybe I had a better chance to play as a true freshman at an even smaller school. That was the main reason I enrolled at Muskingum College in New Concord, Ohio. I actually started a couple of games there as a freshman. After one year I decided that New Concord wasn't for me. It was a little too small. It was hard to get there and hard to get out of there. I called the guy who had tried to recruit me to Dayton, asked if there was any way I could transfer to UD, and I did.

I knew I'd probably be sacrificing playing time because it was going to be a much more competitive situation. Although Dayton was a Division III program at the time (it has since moved up to Division I-AA non-scholarship status), it had just won a national championship and had Division I facilities. Without being disrespectful to Muskingum, Dayton was just a lot more like the programs I wanted to be in. Whether or not I could play there, I wanted to find out.

Whenever my brothers or I would visit my parents in Tampa during Thanksgiving or Christmas break, my mom—who taught second, third and fourth grades during her career—would ask us to stop by her class and see her kids. I'd read a segment of a book or just talk to them. She told her students all about her sons and what kind of little boys we were when we were their age. Making those visits was something we would do not only because our mother wanted us to, but also because it felt good to have a bunch of kids so excited to see us.

One time I watched my mom teach for a day. She was always very, very prepared and seemed very, very thrilled to be with her students—maybe even when that really wasn't the case. Maybe she didn't feel all that cheerful on a particular day, but she was always on her game, always on fire.

"Hello, kids!" she would say, greeting her class with the brightest and cheeriest voice you ever heard. "How's it going?"

Although I never had her for a teacher—with my dad gone all the time with football, my mom left her job for a while to raise us and then returned when we got to sixth and seventh grades—her approach with her students would go something like this: "You got an eighty-seven on that test. That's a good job. Next time get a hundred . . . Ninety-three! Nice job. You're getting there. You're going to get a hundred next time, aren't you?"

There really isn't a whole lot of difference between that and the way I might communicate with a player, like Keyshawn

Johnson, who just helped us win a Super Bowl: "You played pretty good, Keyshawn. You had a heck of a year. Now you've got to be the most dominating sonofabitch ever. You can do that, can't you? You want that, don't you, Keyshawn?"

If there was an elementary schoolteacher who worked more hours than my mom, I'd like to meet him or her. She was grading papers until long after we went to bed. She was up at five o'clock in the morning every day, showing up for work two hours before her students got to class. I know, I know. Like mother, like son. A lot of the assignments she gave her students were creative assignments, which usually meant a lot of extra work for her. She had them writing hardbound books that she would sew together herself. The extent that my mom went to was far beyond the call of duty.

I probably worked out way too much for a third-string Division III college quarterback. I'd lift weights. I'd run. I'd carry a big bag filled with twelve footballs outside and throw them at different targets in my backyard—an old tire hanging from a tree branch or my T-shirt or the nylon mesh ball bag that I'd place in various spots in the grass. I'd make different kinds of throws— on the move, three-step drop, five-step drop, all the different setups that a quarterback does. My parents were in Tampa then. It gets really hot down here in the summer, especially when you're lifting and running and throwing three, four, five hundred balls a day like I was. I was devoted to it. As you can tell by now, if I was going to try anything, it would be full throttle. You don't get anything in life being half-assed.

But I never could get enough football. In the early 1980s, my brother Jay and I would hang out with my dad for about a month at the Bucs training camp. We would throw wide flares and check-downs to the backs during their individual drills or when players would be in town during the offseason working out voluntarily and there wasn't a quarterback around. I'll never forget throwing passes to James Wilder while Hugh Green covered him one-on-one. I'd throw a weak little pass and Hugh would say, "You'd better put some popcorn on that ball!" I would go around at night with my dad on bed check. When the Buccaneers made Blair Kiel, my old friend from Notre Dame, an eleventh-round draft pick in 1984, I spent even more time around One Buc Place in the summer hoping that Blair would make the team. He did for one season.

Being with my dad in that NFL environment was a lot like being with him during those years when he was at Notre Dame. I was having the time of my life. I felt I was on top of the world. That is, until Phil Krueger, who was an assistant to then team owner and president Hugh Culverhouse, started chasing me out of practice. For some reason Phil just didn't like me being around the team. In 1982, my dad's first year with the Buccaneers and my freshman year at Dayton, I was visiting my parents on Christmas break. The NFL had a strike-shortened schedule that year and we were getting ready to play the Bears in what would be the last regular season game. If we win, we're in the playoffs. If we lose, we're out. If we make the playoffs, my dad gets a $6,000 playoff bonus, which means Mom's going to get a new screened-in porch. The Friday before the game, I went over to One Buc Place to watch practice, and Phil Krueger kicked me out. So I went up on the roof of the Hall of Fame Inn, the little hotel that was right next to the practice field, to watch the rest of the workout. Krueger sent a security guy to chase me out of there, too.

At the time, that was all I had outside of school—being a Bucs fan. I would wear my orange Bucs sweatshirt, my dad's Bucs coaching hat, and the Bucs turf shoes that I had gotten from kicker Bill Capece, because his were the only ones small enough to fit me. I thought of myself as a helper for the team. Those were my guys. I loved them. And Phil Krueger wouldn't let me stand there for an hour. My dad couldn't say anything, of course, because Phil was the boss. I'm still mad at Phil for that.

One day in the summer before my sophomore year, I had walked in the house after working out for the fourth time that day. I was sweating. I was flexing. I was looking and feeling like a real stud, man. My brother Jay, who is three years younger, was getting ready to become a junior at Chamberlain High School, where he played quarterback. Jay is tall, six-two. He's about two hundred pounds. He has much more of the physical attributes that you want from a quarterback than I ever had. That's why I got so upset when I found him lying on the couch, watching MTV while munching on microwave popcorn and drinking soda.

"Why don't you get off your ass?" I yelled. "Go outside and work out! You're a bum! You're a BUM!"

If my scolding didn't get through to him, I figured Jay would take one look at me, see the benefits of all of my hard work and dedication and just be shamed right off that couch. He wasn't. So I kept harassing him. I kept challenging him to do what I was doing—to invest the time and effort into making himself a better quarterback and a better athlete.

Finally Jay looked up at me and said, "You wanna race?"

"Yeah, I'll race you," I said.

I assumed it would be no contest. I was a college quarterback who was lifting, running and throwing three and four times a day. Jay was a high school kid who hadn't been off that couch all summer. We would go once around the block in our neighborhood, which was a mile. We were neck-and-neck while jogging practically the whole way. Then as we approached the final two-tenths of a mile, up Old Saybrook Avenue, Jay just left me. He just disappeared like a shot and must have beaten me by 150 yards. I couldn't believe it. When I finally caught up to him he was doing the Rocky Balboa thing in the driveway, running in circles with his arms in the air. I was crushed.

Jay knew I couldn't throw a wet football very well because I have small hands. His hands are big, and he can throw beautiful spirals whether the ball is wet or dry. So at times when it rained he'd go outside with my bag of balls, take them out and start wiping them in the wet grass. "Hey, Muscle Boy!" Jay would yell to me in the house. "Hey, Slappo! You want to come out and throw some footballs? You can't, can you?" He wouldn't let up. He would just kill me and I didn't have much choice but to take it.

Jay would go on to become first-team all-state at Chamberlain. He would go on to the University of Louisville, where he was the all-time leading passer for a while for Howard Schnellenberger. Those were heights I knew I would never reach.

The athletic gap separating Jay and me just served as another reminder that if I wanted to be involved with football beyond college, I'd better take a good look at coaching—that is, after I made as much of a contribution as possible at Dayton. In three years I attempted a grand total of fifteen passes, completing six for thirty-six net yards with one interception. But I did rush for a touchdown in each of those three seasons.

The commitment was driven purely by my love of the game. I wasn't on an athletic scholarship, because Division III schools don't have any to give. From my freshman year my dad made sure that when I came home for the summer I was going to work to help pay for my education. One of the greatest jobs I ever had was the two months I spent working at Hooters on Hillsborough Avenue in Tampa, Florida. That was the second one in the entire chain. I called myself an "independent contractor," because I did a lot of different jobs. I shook wings—mild, medium or hot. I shucked oysters. I changed the kegs of beer. I wiped down tables. I mopped floors. Whatever they needed me to do. As a very proud Hooters alumnus, I still hang out with Ed Drosti, the main man in charge of the franchise, and the rest of the Hooters gang.

I had no problem with the thought of hanging up my helmet

and cleats after my final game at Dayton. I knew I was never going to play this game professionally. I had learned at a fairly young age, in humbling fashion, that I was pretty average at best. I felt satisfied and fortunate that I had the chance to play a full four seasons in college. No regrets. No looking back.

Maybe other guys in that same situation would have kept chasing the dream of making it to the NFL as a player, would have looked around for a tryout camp somewhere, would have wasted a lot of time and energy and money pursuing something that was never going to happen—something that would leave them feeling frustrated and unfulfilled. I just kept my eye on what I felt was a much more realistic target, coaching, without worrying about the road not taken.

In the Dayton football media guide, players had to list their ambition in life. I put down that I wanted to be head coach at Michigan by the time I was thirty-nine. Don't think I'm going to reach that one. Why Michigan? Because at that time I was still that divorced-from-Notre Dame, pissed-off kid, so I wanted to go to Michigan and kick the hell out of Notre Dame. I really wanted to be the head coach at Notre Dame, but at that time I just couldn't make myself state that as an official goal.

Anyone who aspires to be a coach usually majors in physical education, as my dad did at Heidelberg College. I ended up graduating from Dayton with a degree in communications because my dad discouraged me from being a PE major. He was reluctant for me to get into coaching because he knew, firsthand, that maybe it was not all that I thought it was cracked up to be.

"It involves a lot of moving around," my dad told me. "Your fate is not going to be determined by just your performance. It's going to be determined by that odd-shaped ball. It bounces funny ways.

"It's not a job where you're going to have a lot of free time. It involves a lot of hours. So don't put all your eggs in one basket."

It was sound advice. What if I got into coaching and three or four years down the road, I decided I hated it? Now what am I going to be? With a degree in communications, maybe I'd be able to do something in that capacity. I also was kind of interested in going into TV broadcasting, in becoming one of those Curt Gowdys I used to imitate in front of the mirror. I could see myself as a sports anchor or even a writer. I liked creative writing and was pretty good at making up stories. I'm happy to say that this isn't one of them, even if there have been some experiences that seem unreal or almost too good to be true.

I enjoyed studying communications. It forced me to do something that a lot of people—especially young people—don't like to do, which is get up and speak before an audience. I learned all about LOMM—large, open, moving mouth. I learned that it was important to enunciate your words, speak clearly, don't slur. Still, as I've mentioned, my mom always said, "Find your passion." For me it was coaching football. I was never a banner student, but I made damn sure I was solid enough to make it through college because I knew that my lifelong dream was riding on it.

Although I might not have realized it at the time of my graduation, my degree in communications has been helpful throughout my coaching career. It isn't just a matter of being able to express what you think to the media, but also being able to present material to players and other coaches in a classroom-type environment. I understand the value of using visual aids and creative ways to convey your message to stimulate the viewer. I won't just use the standard coaching videotape with sideline and end-zone views. I'll use little highlight clips with music in the background. Sometimes it's old footage. Sometimes it's footage of next week's opponent. Sometimes it's individual, private, off-the-field stuff. But it's always short, always quick, and then we're on to the next thing, which might be looking at an acetate image on the overhead projector or drawings on a grease board or a chalkboard.

That's how I run our meetings, kind of like *The NFL Today* on CBS.

I can't begin to tell you how fortunate I am to have a father who is also my mentor and role model and someone who is always there to give me advice that most guys in this business would kill for. Not only that, but he's also my best friend. You're talking about a guy who has helped me through some difficult situations, personally and professionally—a guy who has enjoyed some of the good times and great times with me. He has been there for every aspect of my football career—as a player and as a coach. We've also sat together at numerous Arena League games, cheering like hell for my brother Jay. One of the reasons my dad wanted to get out of coaching and into the personnel side, first with Tampa Bay and later with San Francisco, was so he could travel and scout college players all over the country and end up wherever Jay was playing for the University of Louisville on Saturdays. He got to see Jay play every game of his college career, which was pretty taxing and quite a sacrifice.

Not much has changed since. Between watching me coach in the fall and winter and Jay play in the spring and summer, I think my dad's been to a football game every weekend the whole year. He told me, "I'm sixty-five years old. I can't take much more of this."

While my dad might have steered me toward a different field of study in college, he did give me plenty of direction on how to become the best coach I could possibly be. He told me that the most direct path I could follow to the top of the business was to become a quarterbacks coach. Even though my dad had spent his career coaching running backs, he knew that a quarterbacks coach usually had the best opportunity to become an offensive coordinator and ultimately be the one calling the plays.

I'm sure that wasn't easy for him to admit, because what he was really telling me was that he wanted me to go further in the business than he had gone. He gave me the road map, the compass and whatever else he could give me to get there.

"If you're going to advance in coaching, you have to learn more about the game than just the running backs," my dad told me. "You want to become a guy that understands protections, understands route distributions, understands the audibles. You were a quarterback. You want to be a guy that has the command of the offense, that can develop people that touch the ball on every play.

"You want to be a quarterbacks coach. And if you want to be a major-college coordinator/head coach kind of guy, you must learn to communicate with the quarterback. And to become the best quarterbacks coach you can be, you need to learn from the best damn quarterbacks coaches in the world.

"Listen to them. Watch them. Study them. Before you're married, while you're young, do whatever you've got to do to get around these kind of coaches."

In 1986, when I was twenty-three years old, that became my mission in life. I was going to go to the football equivalent of Harvard. I was going to grab hold of a branch on the Bill Walsh tree of coaching knowledge that had grown within the San Francisco 49ers. I was going to practically stalk Mike Holmgren, who at the time was the 49ers' quarterbacks coach and one of the best in the business. I was going to find a way to become a great quarterbacks coach myself.

I'm still on that quest.

# FIVE

# Whether You're Cutting Film or Cutting a Rug, You Can't Volunteer Too Much for Knowledge

At Tennessee with Walt Harris, one of my many
great mentors. Baby-sitting his kids was part of
my GA duties. (Courtesy of the author)

**T**HANKS TO MY DAD'S CONNECTIONS I got an interview to become a graduate assistant on the University of Tennessee coaching staff. The Volunteers had one of the greatest offensive minds at the college level in Walt Harris, their offensive coordinator and still one of the topflight coaches in the world.

Walt, who became head coach at the University of Pittsburgh in 1997, was the guru of coaching college quarterbacks at the time. Before joining Johnny Majors's staff at Tennessee he spent three seasons at the University of Illinois, where he developed future NFL quarterbacks Tony Eason, Dave Wilson and Jack Trudeau. Eason and Wilson were first-round picks, while Trudeau was a second-rounder.

Gary Horton, who was one of my dad's scouts when my dad was reassigned from running backs coach to personnel director for the Buccaneers just before John McKay resigned as their head coach, lined up the interview because of a friendship he formed with Walt when they worked together at Illinois. I really owe so much to Gary, who does independent personnel analysis for NFL teams as well as for *The Sporting News*. It's amazing, the people you meet and how they impact your life. I'll never be able to thank Gary enough for helping me get an opportunity to interview at Tennessee. My dad was the one who helped prepare me for it years earlier by having me draw all those circles.

Graduate assistants aren't paid. You get meal money, a place to live, and a minimal amount of living expenses. You're basically a glorified gofer, doing a lot of menial tasks for the coaches but also getting the chance to learn from them and do a little bit of actual coaching yourself. Tennessee had six GA spots—three on offense, three on defense. The way I understood it, under NCAA rules at the time, you could only be a GA for two years. After that it's time to find a job that pays.

To me it sounded like the greatest deal in the world. I was so excited to get behind the wheel of my Pontiac Grand Prix and make that eight-hour drive from Dayton to Knoxville, Tennessee, a place I had known about only from seeing it on TV. The Volunteers had just won the Sugar Bowl, beating the University of Miami 35–7. As soon as you reached the middle of town you could immediately sense the championship atmosphere surrounding the place. When I got there I just found myself staring in awe at this huge structure they called Neyland Stadium.

Following my dad's advice I made sure I got a haircut and brought along a jacket and tie. I also had on a nice pair of brown leather Dingo boots that I thought would just put me over the top as far as my professional appearance. After that it would be a matter of selling myself to Walt, showing him that I would be exactly what he was looking for—a young guy who would work hard, who wouldn't be a pain in his ass, and who maybe was a good coaching prospect. I must have done okay, because I got the job. As for the part about being a good coaching prospect, I can only guess whether Walt actually thought that, considering he never put me on the board. Thank God, because all I could have drawn were circles—beautiful blank circles with no lines. I was like Sergeant Schultz from *Hogan's Heroes*. I knew nothing.

I realized how fortunate I was to be hired. Walt could have gotten anybody he wanted. He could have gotten guys from big-time college programs: Florida, Miami and of course Tennessee. There were a lot of guys who wanted that job, and he ended up picking a Division III backup quarterback—a totally obscure guy with no knowledge about the business. Go figure.

Walt handed me a playbook and told me to be back after I finished school at Dayton. Spring practice at Tennessee would start a couple of weeks later, so UD accelerated my courses to allow me to complete my studies early enough to make it back to Knoxville and be part of spring practice. The playbook, which was three or four inches thick, might as well have been written in a foreign language. It had all these formations and all these words and numbers that I just didn't understand. I thought I was back in one of those dreaded algebra classes.

After returning to Dayton I met my dad—who was in the area while scouting for the Tampa Bay Bucs at the time—on a couple of occasions just to go over the playbook. Even though different teams and coaches use different terminology, it made sense to him. He would recognize a play and then try to explain it to me by converting it to his terminology. "They call this a two hole; we call it a four hole," he told me. "They call this a three technique; we call it a B-gap player."

My dad did his very best to try and explain that "three technique" and "five technique" were references to where a defensive lineman positioned himself in relation to the offensive lineman. The number indicated the alignment to which the defender was shaded. For instance, the outside shoulder of the offensive guard was a "three technique," while the outside shoulder of the offensive tackle was a "five technique."

I still didn't know what the hell he was talking about. And that made me wonder, at least for a moment or two, whether I really was cut out to be a coach. I started to feel overwhelmed. There were four, five, six days when I said to myself, *Maybe I'm in way, way, way over my head.*

Finally I decided I would give coaching a try. I decided that what I didn't know—which was a lot—I was going to learn. I decided that if I worked hard enough at it, if I put in the time and the energy, I could start figuring this stuff out. I decided that I would go after it—that I would burst into this world I knew nothing about with a work ethic that had never been seen. There really wasn't anything for me to lose, because I knew, no matter how well I did in those two years at Tennessee, I wasn't going to begin year three with a full-time spot on the coaching staff or as the offensive coordinator at Florida or the running backs coach at Notre Dame. I was going to have to climb my way up from the bottom.

Being twenty-three and single, I was willing to invest at least the next seven years of my life in finding out if, in fact, coaching was the right career for me. Then I would stop, take a deep breath and see where I had gone and what I had done. In the meantime I wasn't going to let marriage or anything else get in the way of this pursuit. I was all go, go, go, go.

Walt knew that it would take a little time for me to catch on, so he made sure that the assignments he gave me at the beginning were the kind that I could handle. Maybe it was charting plays or running the scout team secondary—introductory duties that I was able to execute while gaining confidence. I also was responsible for coaching the young quarterbacks, and the redshirt freshmen, and for being sort of the offensive coordinator for the jayvee team that Tennessee had at that time. Walt arranged for me to live with the players in the dorm, which would allow me to be kind of his eyes and ears in there and help reinforce some of the points he wanted to get across to the quarterbacks.

Like the rest of the GAs, I served other purposes beyond helping out with day-to-day football stuff. I'd cut Walt's grass, babysit his two kids, drop his wife off at the airport, pick up his mother-in-law when she flew in for a visit, get his car washed and filled with gas, bring him dinner, get him a cup of coffee. They were assignments I could handle. Doing those chores didn't bother me, though, because I was certain that being around Walt and the rest of those coaches would lead to something good. As my dad pointed out, Johnny Majors always surrounded himself with talented coaches. Look at that staff. Besides having Walt as the offensive coordinator, he had as his secondary coach Ron Zook, who in 2002 became the head coach at Florida. His offensive line coach was Phil Fullmer, who became Tennessee's head coach in 1992 and is the winningest coach in Volunteer history. That environment was going to help me get better, but it wasn't a case of Walt or any of the coaches sitting me down and teaching me the offense or any of the basics of coaching. They didn't have time for that. It was up to me to find the answers by asking the right questions and making use of all the great resources that were at my fingertips.

As time went on and I began to show more and more competence and reliability, Walt started to give me more challenging assignments. The biggest was cutting up game film and splicing together specific segments according to the types of plays and situations, and whether they were sideline or end-zone views. Now NFL teams and the bigger college programs have digital-imaging equipment that make this process a whole lot easier and less time-consuming. Back then you had to do it by hand, which took so much longer, even when you knew what you were doing. I learned how to work the splice machine by watching Mike Casteel, a graduate assistant on defense. I became instantly hooked.

Any time of day or night you could find me in the football offices at the Stokley Athletic Center watching film of our games and practices. I'd make cut-ups of pass patterns so I could see a particular play over and over and over. I'd take notes of what Walt would say to the quarterbacks during meetings, and then I'd read them while watching the corresponding play on film. Reading and watching. Watching and reading. Over and over and over.

I did it to enhance my learning. I also did it because whenever I rode in a car with Walt or whenever he invited me to his house for dinner, he would quiz me about football. Our typical conversation would start out about the weather, then maybe shift to his family, then to life in general. At some point, though, I knew Walt was going to get down to business and say, "Okay, Jon, take me through 64 Stay Meyer." It's a pass play that breaks down like this: 64 is the protection, Stay tells the fullback to stay in and block, and Meyer is a basic shallow crossing route.

"How do you coach it?" Walt would ask. "Tell me about the pattern."

The thought of that next car ride or next dinner at Walt's motivated me to make sure I also had a complete understanding of 256 Z Shack and 88 Blue and Green Rip and any other play he might ask me about. Because he was going to ask questions and he was going to find out things I didn't know and he was going to make me get the answers. It was a fantastic learning process, but I was very nervous because Walt was legendary for putting you on the spot with those questions and then humiliating you if you didn't know the answers. That was pressure.

"If you're going to talk to the quarterback, you'd better know what the hell you're talking about," Walt would tell me. "If you're going to help me on game day, you'd better know what I'm talking about."

I'd stay in the offices all day and all night if I had to, because I was on a mission. I wanted to be good. I wanted to be Walt. I wanted to call the plays. I wanted to have that big office he had.

One year Army had ripped us running the wishbone, which is a triple-option offense, and Walt told me to take the film of that game and put together one cut-up of every time they used a veer-block scheme and another cut-up of every time they used a loop-block scheme. There was just one problem: I didn't know what either scheme looked like. Walt didn't have the time to explain them to me, so I found another assistant coach who did, Phil Fullmer. He pointed out that veer and loop schemes are two ways of blocking the point of attack and that the quarterback makes reads as he comes down the line before deciding which of the three options to use: keeping the ball to run it himself, handing it to the fullback or pitching it to the tailback. If the defensive end goes outside, the fullback gets the handoff. If the end slants inside, the quarterback will keep running down the line and read the outside linebacker to decide whether to pitch to the tailback, which he'll do if the linebacker attacks the quarterback. If the linebacker goes outside, he'll keep it and try to turn the corner. The blocking scheme revolves around how the offensive tackle on the side the play is headed gets to the middle linebacker. You can loop outside, around the end, or veer block, which means the tackle comes down inside the end. Either way, he's not going to make contact with the end because that's the quarterback's primary read.

All I had to do after Coach Fullmer's thorough explanation was recognize both blocking schemes on film, which back then wasn't easy for me. Splicing what might have taken an experienced coach forty-five minutes to do took me four hours. I didn't care. The only thing that mattered was that when Walt came in the next morning it was done. I was always nervous when he would put the film on the projector and turn it on. It meant so much to me when he would say, "It's a good cut-up, Jon."

One thing that made pulling those all-nighters a little easier for me than it might have been for someone else was the fact that I didn't require much sleep. My mom and dad will tell you that as a little kid I was always up way before the crack of dawn watching TV or playing board games that usually related to sports in some way. As long as I can remember, I've never slept too much, maybe three or four hours at the most. I've been able to stay up late and still get up early and still feel pretty fresh. It's almost always dark when my alarm clock goes off and I start my day. My wife and three boys are still sleeping as I quietly slip out the back door and head to work. Sometimes the only things awake at that hour are the wild animals outside.

When I was in college I would often spend the whole night reading *Rolling Stone* magazine from cover to cover. Or I'd write letters to anyone I could think of. Or I'd hang out at Timothy's, a bar located three blocks from my apartment and owned by Tony Vitale, a running back who played for my father at Dayton (number twenty-seven, by the way). At one point I thought I had a sleeping disorder and I saw a lot of doctors. I'd be thinking, *Man, I've got to be tired. Damn it, I can't sleep; I'm going to be exhausted tomorrow.* I tried sleeping pills. I even saw a hypnotist one time when I thought about—but never acted upon—being hypnotized so I could sleep more.

Finally I met a doctor who told me, "You have nothing wrong with you. Your physical is fine. You have a gift. There aren't a lot of people who can function perfectly well on minimal sleep. You can, so take advantage of it. You need to find something to do with your free time."

I started collecting baseball and football trading cards. I had volumes of cards that I organized by each player's name and card brand. Then I'd pull out a collector's magazine to see how much my cards were worth, and I'd file the amount with each one. I'd be on my way to becoming a millionaire as I was awake in the middle of the night. I was like Rain Man. On visits to my parents' home in Tampa, I'd get up in the middle of the night and drive to the beach. I'd set up my beach chair in the sand and listen to the crashing waves from the Gulf of Mexico, or I'd just walk around thinking of something to do.

At Tennessee I had plenty to do. If I wasn't already in the office from all day, I'd come to work in the middle of the night. If we played a game, the developed film would be delivered in big orange boxes to Stokley at about nine-thirty or ten o'clock at night. My job would be to splice together the sideline shots of each play on one reel and the end-zone shots on another. The coaches would walk in at six-thirty, seven o'clock in the morning, and everything would be done. It would be as if Santa

Claus and his elves came during the night and delivered the film that way.

"That's a hell of job, Jonny," the assistant coaches would say.

"Yeah, you know, I don't sleep very much," I'd say.

Pretty soon Walt would pile six of those big orange boxes of film on my desk and say, "Let's look at these plays . . . Let's look at this team . . . And after you cut 'em up, we'll look at 'em." It was easy for me to get everything done in the middle of the night because it was quiet. There was nobody bothering me. I'd put my headphones on, listen to a little rock and roll and go to work. I had the best of both worlds: I learned on my own while cutting up the film and then I got to watch the cut-ups with a master.

Before I hooked up with Walt I barely knew that film existed. At Tennessee I was watching professionally made 16-millimeter footage with a sideline and end-zone view of each play. I was watching film of every practice and every drill, as well as of every game. We had 16-millimeter film at Dayton, but we didn't have the kind of budget to film anything besides our games, and the only view we had was from the sideline.

Walt probably wasn't the greatest recruiter in the world at that time, because instead of putting in all the time and travel it took to recruit, he was always in his office watching film. Sometimes he'd be checking out the latest offensive innovations that the 49ers had or Army's veer and loop schemes or San Diego State's unstoppable passing game or Alabama's unbelievable red-zone attack. The man I considered to have the greatest mind in football was always studying the game inside and out in search of something that might stimulate thought about ways he could make his own offense better. He couldn't wait to get his hands on any game or cut-up from any team he could and begin dissecting it for even the tiniest bit of information that might trigger something in his mind.

I'd never seen anyone who loved to study film like Walt

did. He'd watch those reels over and over and over for hours upon hours upon hours. "San Diego State threw for nine hundred yards in three games; watch these three games," he'd tell me. "Geez, you've got to look at this red-zone attack of Alabama."

We had a defensive graduate assistant named Jack Sells who worked for Ron Zook. Ron is the greatest recruiter of all time, so as a GA, Jack was always recruiting, trying to make a name for himself as a recruiter. He excelled at that. He'd get guys to come in on visits. He'd sign guys and strut his stuff and Coach Majors loved him. Me? I was just studying film. I was going to be like Walt. Jack was going to be like Zook. In fact, the other coaches and GAs used to call me "Little Walt" and they used to call Jack "Little Zook." Both are great coaches. They were just different at that time. There are a lot of different ways to skin a cat, man.

There are a lot of different ways to scheme a front, too. It's like fishing in the Gulf of Mexico. You can use different bait for different fish and catch certain fish in shallow water and certain fish out where it's deeper. No matter which way you choose, you can have a hell of a day fishing.

On game day I sat in the press box, right next to Walt Harris. I was responsible for watching out for very specific things from the defense and relaying what I saw to Walt. Different tendencies. Reminders of what we planned to do against certain fronts and coverages. I was just an extra set of eyes for him in the box, but I never actually talked to Walt during a game. For one thing, he was on a headset and I wasn't. For another, he didn't want anything to disrupt his train of thought while he was calling plays. I communicated with him through those little yellow sticky Post-it notes. Whenever I saw something I thought Walt should know about, I would write it down as fast as I could and stick the note in front of him.

In my first year at Tennessee, we were playing Auburn, whose coach at the time was Pat Dye. Auburn was always a bitch to play—Pat's winning percentage was .721 in twelve seasons—and this game was no exception. We had a freeze play, where the quarterback would give a hard count and if he pulled the defense offside, the center would snap the ball, the quarterback would take a knee, and we'd get a free five yards. If the defense didn't jump offside, the quarterback would proceed with a different type of snap count and then run an actual play that he had also called in the huddle along with the "freeze." Auburn's defensive linemen were getting off on the count pretty fast, so I wrote down "Freeze play?" on one of my Post-its and stuck it in front of Walt. Sure enough, the next words Walt spoke into his microphone were, "Let's go with the freeze play." Auburn jumped offside and we got a five-yard gain.

We still ended up getting beat 34–8, but I was feeling pretty good about making that small, positive contribution. I remember driving home from Auburn that night with some of the other GAs, and as soon as we made a bathroom stop, I found a pay phone to call my father. "Did you see that time Auburn jumped offside?" I said, my voice rising with excitement. "I gave Coach Harris a reminder on that play."

The next year, when we played Auburn in Knoxville, I was watching the free safety's depth on play-action passes on crossing routes. I noticed that he was pretty shallow, and I thought that it would allow one of our faster receivers, Terence Cleveland, to get to the post against him. I gave Walt a Post-it that said, "DP8 Go? Check the post." That was a shorter way of saying, "Draw-Pass 8 Go and look for the post route." Walt called the play, and Cleveland caught the ball for a big gain in our 20–20 tie.

Johnny Majors was in a pretty good mood when we watched film the next day. The moment the big pass to Terence appeared on the screen, my heart started beating fast with anticipation. "That's a good call, Walt," Coach Majors said. "That's a good job." I would have been satisfied if it ended right there, but then Coach Harris said, "Jon called that." Coach Majors walked over to where I was sitting, gave me a pat on the back and said, "Attaboy!" That was a highlight of my career. That was one of the greatest days of my life.

I'll never forget Walt for giving me credit on that play. There are a lot of people in his position who wouldn't have done that. There are a lot of people in his position who would have sat there and said, "Thanks, Coach."

It didn't take long for me to discover that coaching wasn't just jogging out there on the field, waving to the crowd with your sweat gear on or yelling at officials. It wasn't that at all. The most important lesson I learned at Tennessee was that you have to have tremendous respect for the game and for the details of the game. Anyone can look and act like a coach, but to actually be one means being able to recognize that this is a good play against this front; this is a bad play against this front. This is a good player; this is a horrible player. This is a defensive guy we should go after with our play calling; this is a guy we should stay away from. These are the rules of recruiting, the lifeblood of your program.

There is just so much to learn about football and there is a never-ending amount of information out there. The respect that I gained for the profession and the knowledge I was beginning to acquire only fueled me to work more hours and learn new plays. I had a wonderful feeling of accomplishment. I felt like I learned a new language. My chest stuck out a little further. I was more confident. I had a sense of belonging.

By spring practice of my second year at Tennessee it all started to click for me mentally. I became really comfortable with the offense and more confident with my understanding of all aspects of it. There were still many things I didn't know, but by then I could tell the difference between a three technique and a five technique. I could draw all the fronts. I could draw all the coverages. I could install the passes and the protections in an elementary fashion for the young quarterbacks I was working with. I could help them call the plays. I could teach them how to use the snap count and how to audible to a run or a pass. I could teach them the formations and protections and where they were supposed to go with the ball against the blitz. I was able to speak like an educated quarterback guy, and I liked that feeling.

I could get on the board or put acetates on the overhead projector and walk the quarterbacks through the different patterns. I was able to do actual coaching with the scout team and the jayvee team. I got to be more productive on game day with Walt in the press box, more comfortable around him and maybe less intimidated.

The quarterback I spent the most time around was Sterling Hinton, a freshman who was on his way to becoming a starter by the end of my second year with the Volunteers. In the spring game he made a couple of right calls on audibles that we had worked on together. It was the first time that I could actually say I helped to accelerate a player's growth, and there was no better feeling in the world. I also spent a lot of time around Jeff Francis, the starting varsity quarterback, and Randy Sanders, his backup, who now is the offensive coordinator at Tennessee. I'd be the buffer between Walt and the quarterbacks, because Walt was hard on those guys. He was just on their asses about everything—from carrying out their play-action fakes properly to looking someone in the eye when they shook hands.

"Everything you have to give, that's what we expect here," Walt would always say. "Don't let that be your claim to fame. We expect that. That's part of the program."

Whenever the quarterbacks screwed up he would let them know. He was like Coach Knight in some ways. He was helping these guys become real men and great technicians and the best quarterbacks they could be, but he was always on their asses.

Mine, too. And we loved it. At night we'd go out for a beer and ask one another, "What did he call you today?"

I didn't have much of a social life at Tennessee. On Saturday nights during the season, if we weren't playing, I'd usually tune in one of Jay's games at Louisville on my car radio. I'd grab something to eat, maybe get a couple of beers, and just go off by myself to listen. I'd have a general idea of what segment of the AM dial the game was on, but I rarely got it on the first try. So I'd keep driving toward Louisville and driving up hills searching for the clearest signal I could find. When I found it, I'd pull over and hear the announcers call the action as Jay put up a ton of yards and a bunch of touchdowns on another opponent. Mentally I felt I was right there with him.

There was one game that Jay played that I didn't have to listen to on the radio. That was when he and the rest of the Louisville Cardinals came to Neyland Stadium in my second year at Tennessee. We were like twenty-five- or thirty-point favorites. The week leading up to that game was tough on me, hearing how our defensive coaches were going to get after Jay's ass. I had heard that kind of talk all the time as our defense prepared for other opposing quarterbacks, but none of those other opposing quarterbacks was my brother. When I talked with Jay on the phone that week and on the field in pregame warm-ups, all we did was wish each other good luck. I sure as hell wasn't going to say, "By the way, bro, the first time you drop back to pass, we're going to bring a corner from the short side to blow your brains out."

During the game, I couldn't help but root for Jay. Blood's thick, man. You want your brother to do well, even when you aren't on the same team. To that point, the last organized sport we had played together was youth baseball in Bloomington, Indiana. Jay had a couple of nice drives in the first half and it was a tight game at halftime. Ken Donahue, our defensive coordinator, was a little bit wary of the young scrapper from Tampa Chamberlain High School. But we got a lead and the Cardinals basically had no chance after that.

As kids, Jay and I were rivals. We would fight all the time, but I was so proud of him when he was tearing it up in college. I still am. Jay is one of the top quarterbacks in Arena Football League history. When the Orlando Predators are at home or in Tampa, I'll usually drop whatever I'm doing and go watch him play. You talk about "Do you love football?" In Super Bowl XXXVII, he's in the press box on the headset with me the whole game, helping me to call plays. And then that night he's on a plane to Chicago to meet up with the Predators for the opening day of the Arena League.

Thankfully, I did take enough time for myself in 1987, just after my second year at Tennessee, to meet Cindy Brooks, who would become my wife. It was the best thing that ever happened to me. Cindy was a Volunteers' cheerleader at the time. She was a beautiful little blond Smoky Mountain girl from the hills of Tennessee. I knew all the cheerleaders. In my mind they were celebrities not just on campus but also throughout the Southeastern Conference.

Cindy had dated John Majors, son of Johnny Majors, for a long time. Then one day at work Todd Fugett, a friend and fellow GA, told me that Cindy and John had broken up.

"How do you know that?" I asked.

"Because I went on a date with her."

I was totally stunned that my man Fugett could get a date with Cindy Brooks. I figured if he could do that, I at least had a chance to talk to her. About a week later I was out at a bar called The Last Lap, on the Cumberland Strip, where all the Tennessee students hang out. Cindy walked in with a couple of her friends. I went up to her and we started talking. Of course I was very nervous. She mentioned that she was having a party at her house the next weekend and she invited me to it.

"If you're serious about this, you can call me and invite me and I'll be there," I told her as I gave her my phone number.

She called me. I went to the party. We became very good friends. We started to date. I started to take a lot of heat around the office from Walt Harris and the other coaches.

Most of the heat actually came from Coach Majors, who could generate plenty of it at any given time. I never worried about the potential risks involved—about the possibility that John Majors could become upset that I was dating his former longtime girlfriend, and that, in turn, might somehow anger his father and I would be out of a job. It never happened, but I didn't care because it was worth the risk. I loved this girl. I would have sacrificed anything, professionally or otherwise, for our relationship to move forward. I knew I was in love with her. I felt that we were going to get married, but first I had to fulfill my vision of what I needed to do to become a good coach. I had the beginnings of a quality education at Tennessee, but I needed to go apply what I learned and then I needed more knowledge. I needed to pay a price to get it, which I knew would likely mean changing jobs and bouncing around the country.

I didn't want to be in a situation where I was luring anyone else into my vagabond lifestyle. My dad and mom were apart a lot during his coaching career, and I kind of wanted to make sure Cindy was willing to be a part of that existence. This is not nine-to-five. This is not punching a clock. This is a different way of life, and I wanted to give her a chance to make sure it was right for her, too. As a newlywed you obviously have to commit yourself to a relationship. I don't think you should get married, go on a three-day honeymoon and then go back to the facility to work all day and all night. I needed to complete my mission first—or at least get a running start on it. I was going to be like one of those monks. I was going to check in and I wasn't going to check out until I felt I was ready.

•

Normally, after the two-year stint as a GA you get a job and get on with your life. I was ready for the second part, but the first part proved a lot tougher than I ever thought it would be. I had trouble just getting an interview for a full-time college coaching position, let alone an offer. I thought for sure that somebody would want me on his staff. With Johnny Majors on my résumé? And Walt Harris? And Tennessee? How could I go wrong?

After we beat Indiana in the Peach Bowl at the end of my second season, I stayed in Atlanta—along with the rest of our coaches—to attend the annual American Football Coaches Association Convention. Walt introduced me to everyone he knew ("Hey, you got anything for this guy?"), but I couldn't get a sniff. I left telephone messages at colleges all over the country. No one would return my calls.

Finally Walt lined up an interview for me at East Tennessee State. I thought I did well, much better than I had done with Walt a couple of years earlier, because I was more knowledgeable and felt a lot more confident. But the job went to someone else. I went back to Tennessee feeling totally depressed.

Although my GA status had expired, Coach Majors offered to keep me on as a "volunteer" coach. Not a lot of GAs received that opportunity, so I felt good that the people in charge of one of the top college football programs in the nation thought I brought some value to their staff— especially when I didn't have any other options at that point. There still wasn't any pay involved, but Coach Majors lined up part-time work for me in what then was the new Thompson-Boling Assembly Center and Arena. I would help straighten up around the facility, set up chairs for concerts, that sort of thing. I wasn't going to give up the hunt for a full-time job coaching football, though.

I knew there had to be another school out there willing to give me an interview. Sure enough, with Walt's help, I found it— Southeast Missouri State University, a Division II program looking for a quarterbacks coach.

I made the six-hour drive from Knoxville to Cape Girardeau, Missouri, and was right on time for my 8 A.M. appointment with Bill Maskill, the head coach. I found out later that even though Bill thought I came across well in the interview, he needed to do a little research before pulling the trigger. He called my high school coach. He called my college coaches, who told him I was a "football junkie." Then he made what, from my perspective, was the best call of them all—to Gary Horton, who once again came to the rescue.

"Billy, if you don't hire him, in two years you will wish you did," Gary told him. "This guy will climb the ladder."

That was all Coach Maskill needed to hear. At twenty-four years old, I officially became a full-time college football assistant coach. I had a $15,000 a year salary. I had a business card. I had everything I could ever want at that stage of my life.

The only problem was that I was hired in April and I wouldn't start getting paid until July 1, when my one-year contract took effect. Southeast Missouri State didn't have enough of an athletic budget to pay me any sooner than that, but I wanted to start coaching right away. I was ready to get together with Phil Meyer, the offensive coordinator, and begin working on the offense that we would be installing for the 1988 season. That meant, from April until July, I had to work a part-time job that the university arranged for me with the Cape Girardeau Public School System. For $6 an hour, twenty hours a week, I was part of a crew that went around town ripping up old carpeting being replaced in schools. It was a bitch of a job, but I had to eat and pay the $150 a month rent for the efficiency apartment I moved into after briefly living in a room that the university paid for at a Budget Motel.

Cape Girardeau gets pretty hot in the spring and summer. It gets even hotter when you're on the top floor of a four-story building, ripping out carpet. Sometimes we had to take chisels and dig the rubber padding off the floor. After a while my hands looked like they were just rotted out. As I ripped through those carpets I kept reminding myself of the only reason I was putting myself through so much abuse. It wasn't for any short-term survival. I could get a job anyplace I wanted for that. It was for the future, for Coach Gruden. I'd be on my hands and knees, ripping and chiseling, and telling myself, *Just keep at it, Coach Gruden. You're getting there, Coach Gruden.*

But the job wasn't finished after you pulled up all the carpet and whatever was left of the padding. Far from it. You had to toss those pieces out of the windows, then go outside, pick them up, throw them into the back of a dump truck, and haul the pile to the dump. Talk about a nasty place. You'd see dead dogs and stinky-ass stuff everywhere.

I'd go home, take a shower and go to the office where Phil Meyer and I would talk about our offense. Phil also had worked with Walt Harris at the University of Illinois, so with that in common we were able to communicate very well.

Phil let me put in a lot of good pass plays that I had learned at Tennessee. Remember, I was Mr. Splice, so I had all of this beautiful, 16-millimeter practice film and game film that came with me from Tennessee. I had cut-ups, I had notes, I had all kinds of stuff for our quarterback, Jim Eustice. When you coach a quarterback you've got to explain what you want him to do. I could very easily explain those passes and those protections to Jim because I had explained them to Sterling Hinton at Tennessee.

Jim threw for 1,800 yards in leading us to a 5–1 record in what was then called the Missouri Intercollegiate Athletic Association, tying us for the conference championship. That was a one-win improvement in our MIAA record the previous season, as the program continued an upturn over some dreadful years from 1980 to 1985. Jim's performance kind of gave me momentum as a quarterback guy. Your players—how well they play, how many games you win—really distinguish a good coaching job from a poor one. I felt I helped Jim. He had some talent, but he was a junior college transfer who hadn't played much before that year and maybe, among the other coaches, he wasn't the most well liked prospect on the team when I got there. He didn't have much mobility. He made questionable decisions. But at the end of spring practice, he had done enough things right to begin winning over the whole coaching staff. When the games started, he got better and better and better.

We just coached Jim the same way that Walt Harris coached Jeff Francis, and like Jeff, Jim bought into what we were teaching him. We graded every play in practice. We yelled and screamed at him. We worked with him on fundamentals and techniques. We gave him tip sheets. We taught him how to recognize fronts and read coverages, how to break down the strengths and weaknesses of a play, how to limit wasted plays with an audible or two. We schooled him up.

I liked the kid because he was smart, and I could see that he could transfer what he saw on the board to the field. He had some talent. He had a good, accurate arm, and he was tough. He just needed to have some success at that period in his life, and we had some patterns I thought just fit him—some disciplined routes, along with some good protection where he could set up and throw the ball.

The highlight of that season was when Murray State, a Division I-AA school from Kentucky, came into Cape Girardeau looking to do some damage to our little Division II program. We were playing out of our league, just filling out their schedule. They had nice, new buses to travel on. They had scholarship players. They had Michael Proctor, a big stallion quarterback who would go on to play in the World League and even spend some time in NFL camps. With the score tied at 13–13 late in the game, Jim led us on a two-minute drive deep into Murray State territory. I was in the press box, on the headset with Phil, who called the plays from the sidelines. Anticipating a blitz and wanting to avoid a sack, I suggested 64 Stubs, an old reliable from Tennessee that called for full protection and a short high-percentage throw to our tight end, Rick Aeilts. Phil called the play, Jim made the throw, Rick caught the ball and, after a chip-shot field goal, we had a stunning 16–13 victory.

It was a terrific sense of accomplishment. You hate to compare anything to winning the Super Bowl, but given the joy that all of us involved with that team felt at that moment it might as well have been. The thrill of victory is all relative.

As a coach I felt I was on schedule, but I also realized that there had to be more things I could bring to Jim Eustice's game. I still didn't know enough. I knew what we had done at Tennessee the previous year, but I kept hearing that Tennessee was doing more things that season and I was missing out on them. That pissed me off.

I would see the Volunteers play on TV and I wouldn't recognize a particular motion or formation. I was still teaching 64 Stay Meyer and 64 Stubs and 64 Oscar and 256 Z Shack and Waggle Right Z Wheel. Yet I didn't see Tennessee running those plays anymore. I saw them growing into a new arena and I wasn't a part of it.

After our season ended Tennessee was playing at Vanderbilt, which was close enough for me to take a drive to see Walt Harris. Once again Walt had me sitting in the press box, helping him just as I had the previous two years. It felt comfortable. It felt right. It felt like I had been reconnected with my past while also plugging into the future. When Walt became head coach at the University of the Pacific in 1989, he saw to it that we could resume working together by offering me a job on his staff.

"You're going to be my tight ends coach, Jon," Walt said.

"Tight ends coach?"

"Yep. It's time for you to learn offensive line play. And the best way for you to do that is to become a tight ends coach."

I was crushed.

"But I want to be the quarterbacks coach, Walt," I said.

"I'm going to coach the quarterbacks, Jon. I need you to coach the tight ends and learn offensive line play."

I knew I had to take the job, because it was a chance to once again work with and learn from one of the greatest coaches around. You just don't pass up an opportunity like that. I also was getting a pay increase from $15,000 to $28,000 per year, and the chance to move from Cape Girardeau, Missouri, to Stockton, California. But all I kept thinking was, *This will not look good on my résumé. All my training was to be a quarterbacks coach. My dad told me to be a quarterbacks coach. The quarterback I had just coached at Southwest Missouri State played well. And what do I have to show for it? A job coaching tight ends.*

Things would only get worse from there. We got our asses kicked that year. We were everybody's homecoming game. We opened up at Pittsburgh, at Arizona, at Auburn, and got crushed in all three games. We were bad. We finished 2–10, making it the worst team I was ever on, record-wise. Pacific, which has since dropped football, was a smaller Division I school, usually playing out of its league competitively. Opponents like Fresno State and San Jose State always had much better players.

The following spring Walt decided to switch from an offense that did a little bit of everything to the run-and-shoot, which was in its heyday at that time. He also switched me to receivers coach, which was fortunate because the tight end is nonexistent in the run-and-shoot. It's wide-open passing, with four or five receivers running routes every play.

Mouse Davis, who was the offensive coordinator of the Detroit Lions, was the leading run-and-shoot expert at the time, and Walt brought him in—along with some assistant coaches at the University of Houston—to speak to us about the finer points of the scheme. It was unlike anything I had ever learned about offensive football, but I understood why we had to do that at Pacific. We couldn't recruit the big-time, feature-horse tailback. We couldn't recruit the big, classic offensive linemen who could come off the ball and thump people. They were going to go to the University of California or Stanford, one of the major programs. California did, however, have a lot of receivers we knew would love to play in a wide-open passing offense. It had a lot of quarterbacks, too. The junior colleges were loaded with guys who could throw and catch the ball, so Walt made the decision to go to the run-and-shoot to allow us to be more competitive.

In theory it was a very exciting offense because the receivers had so much freedom to run the route off the look of the coverage. If you had an out route, it might convert to something else based on the coverage look or how it was played. I was interested in the run-and-shoot, but at the same time I was very concerned about our involvement with it as coaches because the coaches who were using it at that time had their own little clique. Besides Mouse Davis you had June Jones, who, before bringing it to the Atlanta Falcons when he became their head coach in 1994, had coached it as an assistant with the Houston Oilers, and with Davis and John Jenkins when the three were on the staff of the Houston Gamblers of the United States Football League before that.

Walt Harris brought me up in this business. I had studied under him. I also was very aware that the run-and-shoot was catching the football world by storm. It was a great offense, but philosophically I just didn't want to go that route. Walt's decision to switch to it was the right thing to do for that program at that time. But I had my own thoughts on what was the right offense to be associated with, and it wasn't the run-and-shoot, which carried a label that a lot of people coaching in the NFL weren't ready to embrace. I was still on that mission to be connected with Mike Holmgren and learn everything I could about the "West Coast" offense, which I felt was the best in football and the only one for me.

# SIX

# Finding Harvard in San Francisco

## Soaking Up Success and Brainpower with the 49ers

Talking with my dad, my inspiration and guiding light.
(Courtesy of the author)

ONE DAY IN THE SPRING of 1990, the phone rang in Walt Harris's office. It was Mike Holmgren, offensive coordinator of the defending world-champion San Francisco 49ers. Mike was looking to interview me for a position that wasn't even in existence on the 49ers' coaching staff. He wanted a young guy to come in to help him, just be another set of eyes for him, and perform some general coaching/administrative duties, whatever he decided they would be. Although it didn't really have a title beyond "coaches' aide," the job Mike was describing was that of a quality control coach, which few, if any, NFL teams had at the time. He was kind of a pioneer in that respect.

Mike wanted to eliminate some of what he thought was wasted motion when he was in the office. Instead of drawing plays by hand, cutting them out, mounting them on paper, and Xeroxing them off for his players, he wanted to just hand a list of plays to someone, have that person draw them on a computer, and print them out to distribute to the team. That would free up Mike to spend more time studying videotape, coming up with new plays, and just going about his day-to-day chores with greater efficiency.

I didn't really care what I had to do, just as long as I was the one doing it. Every young football coach in America wanted to get in front of Mike Holmgren and have a chance to work for him. He was the hottest offensive coordinator in the business at the time. With George Seifert as head coach, the 49ers had just beaten Denver 55–10 in the Super Bowl. Their "West Coast" offense was in full rhythm. They were exploding on your ass, man.

I should point out that, while I might not have necessarily been counting on it, the call didn't come entirely out of the blue. A few years earlier my dad—after five seasons as director of player personnel and running backs coach with the Bucs—had become a 49ers scout, responsible for the southeast region of the country. Whenever the opportunity presented itself, he would tell Mike about my strong aspirations to join the San Francisco staff so that I could learn the 49er offensive system. He also told him I would be a loyal, hardworking guy who wouldn't overstep any bounds at all. I realize my dad wasn't exactly objective—and I'm sure Mike understood that, too—but every little bit helps.

A second voice that kept putting my name in Mike's ear belonged to Dave Razzano, whose father, the late Tony Razzano, was the legendary head of the 49ers' scouting department from 1979 to 1991. Dave, who was an up and coming scout for the 49ers, had called me one day to say that he had heard of Mike's interest in hiring an assistant who would be willing to do a little bit of everything.

"He's not going to pay much money," Dave warned me.

"I will come there for nothing," I said. "Tell Coach Holmgren I'll pay him to take the job."

I was serious about that. After the interview I sat on pins and needles for two or three weeks, waiting for Mike to call. One day, sure as hell, the phone rang. It was the call I was waiting for my whole life up to that point.

"You've got the job," Mike said.

At the time it was my biggest break. I saw it as the beginning of learning relentlessly for the next four or five years in an offensive system that I truly believe is the best that I've ever seen.

I immediately called my dad. He was happy for me, but he also gave me the following advice: "Just work your ass off, but don't let your ambition get in the way of the respect for what these people have done—what you have not been a part of. Don't be offended if you're not invited to do certain things. It isn't personal; it's just the way it is. Remember that you're a fly on the wall. Watch. Learn. But don't irritate them or they'll swat you with one of those little fly swatters, and you'll be dead."

I didn't lose sight of the fact that I wasn't just representing myself with the 49ers. I was representing my dad as well. By recommending me as strongly as he did, he had put his reputation on the line with a team that had employed him for three years up to that point. I knew he trusted me and was confident I wasn't going to do anything to embarrass him or myself.

Walt tried to talk me into staying at Pacific. He wanted me to be part of the vast improvement he knew that the run-and-shoot would bring to the program at that time. And, by God, eventually it did. That fall, Pacific would have some unbelievable offensive output and even set some NCAA records, but deep down I think Walt knew I had to jump on this offer. The 49ers were always Walt's vision of the perfect offense. From day one at Tennessee, he would do anything he could to get his hands on 49er film. He also had advised me more than once to do whatever I could do to go to San Francisco.

But I could never forget all that Walt has done for me. He is the one who got me started. He is the one who showed me the benefits of hard work and how to maximize my productivity. He is the one who taught me how to study football, that it isn't just a matter of sitting in a room and looking at tape. He taught me that you have to watch situational football—red zone, goal line, short yardage—and that there are certain teams you have to look at and why you're looking at them. He taught me how to research opponents, how to put together game plans, how to be thorough, how to coach a young quarterback. If I had a chance to just float down a river in a boat and talk about football and talk about life, he'd be the guy I would call.

At Pacific I was making $28,000 a year. I had free use of a new car from a local dealership. I had a nice little apartment in Stockton. How much did I want to work for the 49ers? I accepted a salary of $800 a month, about a third of what I was making at Pacific, with no contract. I bought a small, unfurnished efficiency apartment. I didn't have a car, so I rode my bike to work. When I worked late (which was most of the time), rather than try to make the long bike ride home in the dark, I would just sleep at the team's training facility and office complex. Not that that was a horrible experience or anything. Team owner Eddie DeBartolo, Jr., spared no expense in building the Marie P. DeBartolo Sports Centre, named in honor of his mother. The place was like the Taj Mahal. It was a two-story, 52,000-square-foot building that sat on eleven acres. It had a state-of-the-art fitness room, a thirty-foot-by-forty-foot hydrotherapy indoor swimming pool, racquetball courts, a whole bunch of meeting rooms, and all other amenities to make for the most comfortable and productive work environment for players, coaches, staff and media. I'd sleep in a room adjacent to the giant office of Eddie DeBartolo, Jr. It had a refrigerator, a TV and a nice, comfortable couch. He was fine with that, and the best part was I didn't have to make the bed in the morning.

The 49ers' image was just stunning. They were on the cutting edge in every phase of football. Everything they did wasn't first class; it was above that. They had great coaches and players. They had Joe Montana at quarterback, Steve Young at backup quarterback. They had Jerry Rice in his prime, when he was really heating it up, when that fastball was two hundred miles an hour. They had John Taylor, Roger Craig, Tom Rathman, Brent Jones. They had guys who understood the system and who knew the responsibility they had to dominate. They were coming off back-to-back Super Bowls, and Eddie DeBartolo was going to make sure they had every reason to win the next one—the best coaches, the best players, the best facilities, along with the right kind of morale and chemistry to produce a winning attitude.

All I wanted to do there was take advantage of the opportunity.

When I first got the job, I had never even turned on a computer. Now I had one on my desk. I was expected to learn how to work it and how to draw up plays on it while Mike and all the other coaches went on summer vacation for a month. I was nervous. Suzette Cox, who was Mike's secretary, stuck around to teach me how to use the computer, but I wasn't the best student. Maybe that was why we didn't hit it off really well. I admit, I could have had a little better attitude, but there I was, ready to soak up this seemingly endless supply of football knowledge from the San Francisco 49ers, and they've got me sitting in an office learning how to use Super Paint 1.0. Guys from the Silicon Valley also came by to show me how to draw a play, how to save it, and how to store it. It was a long, hard process for someone who was completely computer illiterate.

Drawing plays for the 49er offense, in which you could run the same play three hundred different ways, made it that much tougher. You could have Brown Right A Right or Y Shift to Brown Right A Right. You could have Blue Right E Motion or Blue Right E Counter Motion. You could have a whole dozen separate drawings of just 2 Jet Flanker Drive. All summer I'd walk in there at four or five in the morning, draw day and night until I collapsed, then come back the next day to draw some more.

After a while I started getting pretty good on the computer. Once I learned my way around the building, I started checking out the amazing library of information there. It was a football coach's gold mine. The 49ers not only have all the game plans of the Bill Walsh era saved; they also have all of the videotape of Bill Walsh and his assistant coaches installing offensive plays with the players at training camp. When I wasn't sitting in front of my computer, I'd go into an empty meeting room with a blank notebook and watch Coach Walsh install 200 Jet X Slant or the late Bobb McKittrick, who was still the offensive line coach when I was there, install 17 Bim and 19 Handoff Crack and 19 W.

Then, on the computer, I set up my own private files of plays and concepts of things that I liked. For instance, I'd enter "16 Power" or "25 Protection" and type in the notes I had heard Bobb say about them. Later I would add files of things Mike Holmgren would say in offensive meetings and everything George Seifert would say to the whole team.

When I was at Tennessee Mike was the quarterbacks coach for LaVell Edwards at Brigham Young University. He was coaching guys like Steve Young and Marc Wilson in an offense that was throwing for eight hundred yards a game. He helped BYU win a national championship in 1984. But two years later, when Mike left to coach quarterbacks for San Francisco, he was under the gun because now he was working for Bill Walsh, the master-mind of offensive football. You talk about heat.

Yet Mike handled it well. The fact he had been a high school teacher and was so comfortable in his ability to communicate with players helped him tremendously. Mike could take something that was very sophisticated, very complex, and present it in a simple, basic fashion that even I could understand it—and I was new there. It wasn't a forty-five-minute lecture. He had a knack for conveying his thoughts in twenty-five words or less. He didn't start rambling and talking about things that were irrelevant to the question that you had just asked. He was always to the point.

When Mike installed plays, he never left any doubt about what players had to do or how they were supposed to do it. There were no gray areas in his presentation. He was the same way when he worked with his quarterbacks. It wasn't like a golf lesson where you go out there and pretty soon you've got so many coaching points, you can't even take the club back. Mike wouldn't go into a detailed critique about Joe Montana's footwork or stance. He would just say, "Joe, you're okay getting away from the center. Stretch your drop. Your drops are too shallow." That's all Joe needed to hear. It was very cut-and-dried, which kind of surprised me, because everything I had seen the 49ers do was so precise, their execution was so extraordinary, I just assumed Mike had to spend countless hours on basic, fundamental technique-type things.

At six-foot-five, Mike is quite an imposing figure. When he installs a game plan, showing each play and its corresponding number on the overhead projector, he always exudes confidence.

"Picture Number 73 is going to be a touchdown Sunday," he'd say matter-of-factly, about a pass play designed to have Joe throw to Jerry Rice, who would just blow past some poor DB trying to cover him one-on-one over the middle. "Pay attention, men. It's 76 X Shallow Cross. Roger's going in motion to the weak side. The free safety is going to jump the tight end on the hook route, and Jerry Rice is going to be there for a touchdown. It's going to happen, men. Circle it now. Star it. It's a touchdown."

I would sit there and go, "Man, it's seven to nothing already. What's the next picture?"

But that's how you install plays. Confident. Concise. Crystal-clear. No one does it better than Mike Holmgren.

One of the few strengths I know I have is judging a situation when it is time for me to disappear. That would usually be the case in the quarterback meetings or wherever Mike was talking one-on-one with Joe Montana, the greatest quarterback and best and baddest dude of all time.

I felt that the Holmgren-Montana relationship was private—or at least should have been treated as such—and I didn't want to infringe on it. I wasn't there for the previous two years when they won Super Bowls, and I kind of felt like some of the things they were talking about were a little bit personal. They didn't know me, so there was no reason for them to think that I could be trusted to hear those kinds of conversations. I'd be wondering if, when Joe spoke about certain topics, he was thinking, *Man, I hope this guy doesn't go tell John Taylor that I didn't like his route on the Dino in the red zone.* The last thing I wanted to do was have either one of them feel awkward because of my ass sitting in there.

It also was a little bit awkward because Steve Young, who had joined the 49ers a few years earlier in a trade with Tampa, was a very frustrated backup at that time. We had known each other while Steve played quarterback for the Buccaneers when my dad was their personnel director. My dad had a little bit— not a lot, but a little bit—to do with the Bucs acquiring Steve out of the USFL with the first pick of a supplemental draft in 1984. Steve had some rough times in Tampa, but I can't imagine him being any unhappier than he was at that time in San Francisco. He was always clashing with Mike. Now, remember, Mike coached Steve at BYU. They had a lot of success together and they were best friends, but Steve was so frustrated because here was this well-lubricated machine that was just rocking with Joe out there, and Steve was on the sideline just watching, cheering.

Steve was a truly great player himself. He had the talent to be an outstanding quarterback, which was obvious to anyone who saw him play. He was a good enough athlete that he probably could have held his own at some other positions, but he wasn't even holding for extra points. He seemed to feel hopeless about the whole situation.

"I'm never going to play here," Steve would say.

Then he'd start lobbying to get on the field any way he could: "I want to be a receiver . . . I want to be a gunner on the punt team." Actually, Steve did end up playing in a couple of games as a fourth receiver, although he didn't have any catches. That did nothing to make his situation any more bearable or to ease the tension between him and Mike. Finally Holmgren came to me one day and said, "I'm done with him. You coach him."

"Really?" I said. "Okay."

I knew Mike wasn't actually putting me in charge of Steve Young; that was still Mike's job. But I saw the fact he was letting me help him out a little bit as a tremendous responsibility, because for the first time in my life I would be working directly with an NFL quarterback. I would be doing some actual coaching. Even if Steve almost never saw the field, it was my job to help Mike in helping Steve be ready to play in every game, just in case Joe got hurt. Steve and I would meet late in the week to go over the game plan. I would give him quizzes to help him remember all of those 150 pass plays in there. I also would give him all the encouragement I could.

"You're going to get your chance," I said. "You're going to play great. Why are you here? Why don't you just have your agent trade your ass? I know why. Because you want to be the quarterback of the 49ers."

Steve began to trust that I was genuinely interested in seeing him improve and land the dream job that was only a heartbeat away, even if it seemed so much further than that. With Joe headed for a second straight league MVP award, the distance might as well have been measured in light years.

The 49ers were as dominant as ever that season. We had a 13–1 record going into our last two games. We already were the NFC Western champions and had a first-round bye for the playoffs. Joe was bothered by a lower abdomen strain, so he wasn't even in uniform for our next-to-last game, against New Orleans. Steve got the start, and even though we ended up losing, he ran for 102 yards, making him only the second quarterback in 49er history to rush for more than 100 yards in a game. For the regular-season finale in Minnesota, the plan was to let

Joe start and play the first half, so that he would get some tune-up work for the playoffs, then let Steve play the second half. The Vikings had a good team. They had some talented players on defense—Chris Doleman, Keith Millard, Carl Lee—and held a 10–0 lead at halftime.

I knew Steve had some concerns as we stood on the sidelines just before he would enter the game at the start of the third quarter.

"What do you think, bro?" he said.

"You're going to kick ass, man," I told him. "You're going to kick ass."

I wasn't in any position to offer him much more than a little encouragement, because I wasn't involved with any of the sideline communication with the quarterback. Mike and the other position coaches handled that. On game day my two main responsibilities were to be the "get-back coach" and to help out our special teams coach, Lynn Styles, with substitutions. Every team has a "get-back coach," whose job is to constantly tell all the people on your sideline to "get back" behind the designated borderlines for coaches and players so that the team doesn't get a five-yard penalty.

The officials make a big deal before the game of reminding both head coaches where everyone is supposed to stand, and that absolutely no one besides their players is to be on the field. When that happens, the officials get pissed, because they want a completely clear path so they can run up and down the sides of the field without having to take their eyes off the action. And, without fail, it happens at least once, causing the side judge or the referee to yell to the head coach, "You'd better tell these players to get back!" Coach Seifert would yell, "Gruden! Get these guys back!" Usually it's never the starters inching their way toward the field. It's almost always the third corner, the nickel back, the extra linebacker—situational substitutes waiting their turn to go into the game. But whenever I'd go tell them to get back, they'd tell me, "Shut up, man. Get out of my face."

On third down I would have to yell, "Punt return alert" or "Punt alert," so that Lynn's guys would be ready to go into the game. If someone playing special teams got hurt, I had to make sure the backup knew that he was "L-3" (third man in from the sideline to the kicker's left) or "R-4" (fourth man in from the sideline to the kicker's right), on the kickoff-coverage team, or the right guard on the punt team. "You'd better be ready," I'd warn them. Of course they, too, would tell me to shut up and get out of their face.

Against the Vikings Steve ended up throwing his first touchdown pass of the season, a fourteen-yarder to Jerry Rice, midway through the fourth quarter. With the Vikings still up by four points, Steve ran a beautiful two-minute drill. He hit six of seven passes, including a thirty-four-yard strike over the middle that John Taylor caught for a touchdown with twenty-nine seconds left. We end up winning the game 20–17 and finishing with a 14–2 record. On the plane ride from Minnesota I was sitting alone, as usual, going over my notes. All of a sudden offensive lineman Harris Barton came up and said, "Hey, bro, Steve and I are going out tonight and you're going with us." I couldn't believe it. You talk about a big-time deal: I was invited out to a fancy restaurant with Steve Young and Harris Barton—and they were buying. It doesn't get much cooler than that.

Later I did kind of get a little bit uncomfortable, wondering if Joe maybe thought I was kissing Steve's butt. That wasn't the case at all, and in the long run it really didn't matter. Steve felt good about what he had accomplished in that game, and he wanted to show his appreciation.

To this day, that story about Steve helps me in dealing with backup players who want to be starters and believe that the only way to get there is on another team. "If you're in a place you want to be and you're in a system you want to be in, don't underestimate that," I'll say. "Wait your turn. I've seen a guy do that. Sure enough, when Joe Montana got hurt, Steve Young lit it up, man. Now Steve Young is on his way to getting into the Hall of Fame."

The biggest thing Mike wanted to accomplish each week was to make sure that Joe liked the plays that Mike would be calling on Sunday. Mike wanted to make sure that Joe felt good about the game plan. As a coach, you're going to change formations and add new plays, but you'd better make sure that your quarterback is sold on what you're doing. That's what all coaches are—salesmen. You've heard a coach say after a loss, "Well, we had a hell of a plan. We just didn't execute it." What he's really saying is, "We probably didn't execute it because our players didn't understand it, and they made mistakes." If the players didn't understand it, chances are they didn't like it, which means the coach didn't do a good enough job of selling it.

If you've worked on that game plan all night on Monday and Tuesday, when you walk into that first big meeting of the week with your offense on Wednesday, you want it to get their attention. You want them to like it. You want them to be excited about it. So Mike would hit Joe with an endless barrage of questions: "Do you like Waggle Right Double Out Waggle Right Drag Hook? Do you like it? Do you feel good about the setup?" If Joe nodded his head, Mike would say, "Okay, good. How do you feel about the audibles that are accessible to you in the blitz this week? Do you feel good about those?"

I do the same thing when I'm going over the script of our first fifteen plays. I'll ask Brad Johnson, "Do you like 22 Z In? What do you give it on a scale of one to five?" If he gives it a four, I'll write that on my practice script, which reminds me that this is a play he likes a lot and therefore I'm more likely to call it.

"What about 72 X Shallow Cross? One to five?" Now if he says "three," I might question his sanity because I know it's a good play. But I won't try to convince him to like it as much as I do because if he doesn't feel comfortable with a play, that's probably going to show up in the execution. Once I hear a three or a two from the quarterback, I'll never call the play. If there are two or three plays he doesn't like, it's not a problem. We've still got 147 others from which to choose.

Another thing I learned from Mike is that having favorite plays is a two-way street. A lot of times there are plays that players want you to call, but just hearing them tell you how much they like it isn't enough reason to call it. You have to see proof in the way they practice it. It isn't like you have time to practice Waggle Right Double Out twelve times or 22 Texas sixteen times. You practice each one maybe twice. Mike would let the players know that the onus was on them to make the plays they wanted to run on Sunday look good on Wednesday, Thursday and Friday.

"Do you guys like this play?" Holmgren would say in a challenging tone. "It's the sixth play of seven-on-seven today and it's the ninth play of the team period, so it had better look good or you're not going to get it called during the game."

Guys would compete with that in mind.

George Seifert was in his second year as the 49ers' head coach, having been promoted from defensive coordinator after Bill Walsh retired. George had the most organized practices I had ever seen. Everything was situational. It wasn't just a case of "Let's go out here and run some plays." It was "We're in the red-zone fringe here. We've got five shots from the twenty-five, we've got three from the twenty, two from the fifteen, two from the ten, and two third-and-goals from the three."

He didn't want his team spending any more time on the practice field than it had to. When the horn blew to end one period, the next period had better be set up and ready to go. It was tight. It was precise. The "look squad"—which is another name for the scout team because it provided the offense or defense with the "look" of the opponent's offense and defense—was coached as hard as the regulars. George demanded the perfect look. So if, for instance, the guy emulating Junior Seau didn't bite on a play fake, you'd hear "Damn it! Junior Seau's not going to play like that. He's going to bite on the play-action pass. He's Junior Seau. He bites on everything. We need more activity. Bite on a play pass! We're trying to get that ball thrown in behind you!"

George had a very low tolerance for error. If a play wasn't run properly, it was repeated at the end of practice. He'd tell Mike, "I need to see play number nine again . . . I need to see number eleven one more time." Everybody would be pissed when that happened, of course, because when you repeat plays it makes the practice longer. There would be a lot of days during the season when the players practiced without pads or in pads and shorts so they wouldn't be beating on each other and getting too worn out to be effective late in games or late in the season. But they still practiced with speed and explosion.

George had a beautiful office that was always neat, nothing out of place. That was because the place where he actually did all his work was a little room connected to that office. George had his projector in there and a bucket stuffed with about a hundred number-two pencils all sharpened to a razor-point edge. It was like his laboratory and George was like a mad scientist. One night when George wasn't around, I walked in there and saw that he had drawn plays and made a bunch of notes on four or five writing tablets. He was working his ass off on all aspects of the team. There were eraser shavings everywhere, offensive and defensive tapes all over the place, and I noticed that a lot of those pencils were as dull as a butter knife. I thought I would help the head coach out a little bit, so I took each dull pencil, put it into an electric sharpener to restore that razor sharpness, then put it back into the bucket. I cleaned off the eraser shavings and stacked up his tablets.

Much to my surprise, an angry George began the next day's staff meeting with a question: "Who messed with my office?"

"I did, Coach," I said, instantly realizing that my good intentions had turned into a very bad mistake.

"Don't you EVER go in there and touch my stuff again."

"Yes, sir."

So much for being that fly on the wall my dad talked about.

George would watch all the film of each opponent—every bit of offensive and defensive film—and would form his own opinions that didn't always agree with what his assistants thought. Sometimes, before we hit the field, George would take the cards that showed the scout team defense how the opposing defense was supposed to line up in practice and change them to how he thought it was going to align. When practice began Mike Holmgren and Joe Montana would see the revised card, and they wouldn't like it.

"Who did this card?" they would say. "They're not going to play that coverage."

"Oh yes, they are," George would shoot back. "I've been watching them all week. They're not going to line up and just let you gut them. They're going to do it this way."

I spent a lot of time helping Mike, but I'd also be involved in different drills on the practice field. As soon as the prepractice stretching was over, I'd go over to help the secondary coach, Ray Rhodes, in period one. I'd throw balls so the DBs could work on their interception skills. Some were low, some high, some in the hole between the safeties and corners. I used be as nervous as hell throwing to Ronnie Lott and Eric Wright and Chet Brooks, because I knew if I threw a bad ball, I was going to hear about it from them. Coaches also made sure I was doing the drill the way they wanted it done.

"Put a little mustard on it!" George would bark. "Goddamn it, throw a higher ball! . . . Throw a lower ball!"

Ray was the ultimate, consummate players' coach. All the players loved him, offensive guys as well as defensive guys. The DBs liked going to his meetings. They couldn't wait to hear Ray Bob, which was what they called him, although I have no idea why. Ray had an unbelievable way of communicating with the players. He'd get on your ass and then he'd make you laugh, all in the same sentence. It was the exact opposite of any other meeting I had ever attended. I'd like to share what Ray told his players, but if I did, this book would get an X rating. His language was as raw and as salty as could be. That's where I learned a lot of the colorful phrases I use to this day. Ray Bob would say just about anything to get his points across. I didn't know you could talk like that without getting put in jail.

One time after a meeting, I asked him, "How do you even think of those things that you say?"

"Hey, you can say it like it is or say it like it isn't, Gruddog," Ray said. "Some of the more descriptive adjectives we use have four letters to them."

Don't get me wrong. Ray conveyed a lot of technical football in his meetings, but in the middle of watching tape he would go off on some pretty graphic tangents. The bottom line was that Ray knew how to reach players, how to keep their attention, which is half the battle in these meetings.

Being a secondary coach for an accomplished defensive guy like George Seifert isn't easy. That's like being a quarterbacks coach for Bill Walsh. But Ray Bob was one of the best field coaches I've ever seen. Besides getting to see him in action while throwing balls to his DBs in practice and pregame warm-ups, I would always make a point of getting together with him during training camp, at lunch or in the evening, and ask him how certain plays we were using on offense look from a defensive perspective.

"Does this play hurt this coverage?" I'd ask him. "Does that play hurt this coverage? Do you feel you can stop this play with that coverage?"

After finishing with the DBs, I'd go over and chart plays for Mike, then, in period three, I'd serve as the quarterback for one-on-one pass-rush drills involving the defensive and offensive linemen. Bobb McKittrick would actually have me call the play in the huddle so his offensive linemen would hear what the protection sounded like under circumstances similar to the way they would hear it in a game. He didn't just want to send them up to the line of scrimmage and say, "Okay, it's you against you. Ready, set, hut." We'd get in the huddle and I had to call the play just like Joe Montana did: "Red Right 22 Z In! . . . Blue Right F Short 2 Jet Flanker Drive . . . Red Left F Short 3 Jet Flanker Drive Halfback Corner . . . Change Right C Left 72 X Shallow Cross." I had to give the snap count: "On one . . . On two . . . On first sound." Once I got up to the line, I'd say the cadence just like I heard the quarterbacks do it: "Blue 85 . . . Blue 85 . . . 34 . . . Set, hut!"

The center would hike the ball, I'd drop back to pass, and the defensive linemen would rush. We're talking about Charles Haley and three of the best nose tackles in the game—Michael Carter, Jim Burt and Fred Smerlas. Fortunately the same hands-off policy that applied to Joe and the other quarterbacks applied to me, too. Thank God.

Bobb McKittrick is the greatest coach I've ever seen. He is my all-time coaching idol. Bobb was bald and had dark eyebrows. He looked like Captain Jean-Luc Picard of the Starship *Enterprise*. For a guy in his mid-fifties, Bobb was in top physical shape. He was an ex-marine and he was buff—buff and tough. Whether it was a hundred degrees or cold as hell, he would always wear a short-sleeved shirt and a fishing hat.

He might have been the most respected coach on that 49er

staff. I can't tell you how many times Coach Seifert would go up to him and ask, "How do we help on blocking this guy? What do you think of this? What do you think of that?" Bobb had bizarre intelligence that he was able to apply to the players. He knew the strengths and weaknesses of every defensive front. Among the many valuable lessons he taught me was that it's one thing to identify the front; it's another thing to identify the talent level of the personnel within the front. I was always amazed at how, in every game, Bobb could carry thirty-seven different runs and twenty-five or thirty different pass protections. He also was brilliant in terms of self-scouting, where you study your own tendencies to make sure you're not becoming too predictable to the opponent with the plays you call, when you call them, and the formations you use. He'd have running plays out of formations we had only passed from previously. There would always be some tendency breakers. "We've run 200 Jet X Slant six times," he'd say. "It's time for Blue Right F Short 65 Charlie."

You had to ask yourself, *How in the hell do you coach all those runs and protections to five guys in four days?* Bobb would find a way. He would spend hours breaking down all his own film and drawing every run and every protection by hand. I used to just marvel at the guy's stamina. I would say, "Bobb, you need any help, man? You need some water? Can I get you anything to eat? How about a biscuit?" He'd just shake his head and keep on working. I don't know how he did it.

Mike's meeting room was right across the hall from McKittrick's office. I was in Mike's meetings all through training camp, but a lot of times during the season I would slide out of those quarterback sessions and go over to Bobb's meetings, which normally lasted a lot longer. With all those extra-large bodies, there usually wasn't enough room for another person in there, but Bobb kept the door open and I would just sit outside and take notes. The amount of knowledge he had was unbelievable. I'd get fourteen, fifteen pages of notes out of one forty-five-minute meeting that he had with his linemen. Through that whole meeting those guys would be leaning forward, eyes wide open, because Bobb knew how to keep it interesting, and they knew that if they paid attention, he was going to make them better players.

When the meeting was over, I'd go help Bobb clean up his office. "That was the damnedest meeting I've ever seen," I would say. I'd have a litany of questions for Bobb, but I was always conscious of bothering the coaches. I figured right after a meeting they would be tired or they would want to get on to their next assignment or they just didn't have the time. But Bobb knew I was really inquisitive and that I was very anxious to see his interpretation of the world. Sometimes he'd actually go out of his way to say, "I know you have questions. What are your questions?"

As smart as Bobb was, he had a real humbleness about him. When pointing out mistakes in practice, he wouldn't take a direct shot at the players. Instead he would belittle himself. "If we put this on film, I won't even be able to afford to eat at Jack in the Box," he would say. "As a matter of fact, I'll have to go to all-you-can-eat at Ponderosa or Shoney's, just so I can get one meal a day, one meal a week." ·

Bobb was the same guy every day. He was never yelling. He was never up or down. He was always steady. And he would work with anybody, even if the guy had no chance to make the team. You could pretty much tell who had a chance to make the 49er team. You knew they were going to keep eight linemen and the rest of the seven guys were long shots, yet Bobb would work with the fifteenth guy like he was the first guy. Players respected him for that.

Bobb had the respect of a lot of people around the league, except for defensive linemen. They hated him for the chop blocking and cut blocking he had his linemen do before players were fined for every down block they made. Hell, he had them cross-body blocking people. Bobb would always tell his guys, "You block back high, you block down low . . . and if he's wearing a knee brace, bend it." The linemen would all laugh, but Bobb was serious.

The information I got from him and his meetings came in handy when I would go over the game plan with Steve Young. To help Steve with the learning process, I'd play a game of Twenty Questions with him. For each one Steve answered wrong, I got a point. For each right answer, he got a point. One time he began the game by getting twelve right answers in a row, so I decided to reach a little deeper into my knowledge pool.

"Okay, Steve, if it's a 38 F, and they play a 59 defense, what's the right tackle's call?" I asked.

"What the hell you talking about?" Steve said.

"That's the question. It's in the game plan. I get the point."

I know what you're thinking. How can someone who aspired to be a quarterbacks coach and an offensive coordinator, a guy who was always told that that was the career path to follow, gravitate to an offensive line coach? It all goes back to Walt Harris. When I was at Pacific he made me learn about the tackles, tight ends, blocking combinations and protection responsibilities. When I had to sit in on all those offensive line meetings, I learned a whole new wealth of information. I began to see a much bigger picture of the offense, and I realized how important that would be in the future. Once I became a coordinator, I wanted to be able to communicate with the offensive line coach. I wanted to be able to speak the same language, to understand what he understood. I knew that it was vital to have a top-notch offensive line coach who is going to give you a strong opinion because that's his expertise. Show me a championship team and I'll show you a stud of an offensive line coach on the staff, such as Bobb McKittrick in San Francisco, Tom

Lovat in Green Bay, Alex Gibbs in Denver and our own Bill Muir in Tampa Bay. At the same time, you don't always want to have to agree with your line coach just because you lack the knowledge to have an opinion of your own.

By studying offensive-line play, I was able to learn a whole new perspective of football. Forget about going to coaching clinics and watching and listening while some guy draws up routes. I wanted to know, "How did you keep that great speed-rushing end out of your backfield? How did you let your quarterback take a seven-step drop and still throw the ball? How do you get five guys into a route? What if they bring two blitzers from over there and two from over there? Where do you go with the ball? What happens when this linebacker stems in the A gap? Is it a hard call? Is it a gap call?"

I wanted to learn the nuances of the protections and of the blocking schemes. I wanted to be able to have the authority to walk into any meeting of the offensive football team, whether it be with the running backs or with the tight ends, and understand exactly what was being discussed. When you know what the hell you're talking about in every phase of offensive or defensive football, it gives you more respect with the players involved. When Brad Johnson is throwing passes in practice to Keyshawn Johnson and Keenan McCardell, you don't stand there and say, "Gee, Brad, nice throw! Super job! Nice catch, Keyshawn! Great throw, Brad! Nice catch, Keenan!" That's not coaching. That's cheerleading.

If you're going to be a coordinator, you have to coordinate the entire offense. You bring your staff together and you recognize everything about the team you're going to play—the personnel, the fronts. You're the one who goes around the table in a staff meeting and says, "You bring your ideas to the table, you bring your ideas to the table. Let's adjust the problems, let's react to what we see here, and I'll make the final call." You have to assume the responsibility of determining what your offense is going to do in the end, but to make the final call, you'd better know what the hell you're talking about and you'd better have a staff with a lot of ideas.

Even after I went on to Green Bay, Philadelphia and Oakland, I'd always make a point to find Bobb McKittrick when we would be at the same event where NFL coaches always gather in the offseason, like the Scouting Combine at Indianapolis or the Senior Bowl college-star game in Mobile, Alabama. I'd sit right next to him as he was watching the offensive linemen work out. I'd start bombarding him with about thirty questions. "You guys were playing Cincinnati last year against the 34 defense, and you were fanning the backside of your protection," I'd say. "Was that a rule or was that an adjustment?" Bobb would say, "Do you watch any of your film or are you just watching all of our films?" But he would answer my questions, and I think he used to appreciate that I was so interested in him and what he was doing. Bobb was my guru. He was my guy.

I spoke with him a lot by phone. He called me all the time in 1998, my first season with the Raiders. He would maybe critique something he saw or say something he felt needed to be said. One day he called after a victory. He talked about our game and congratulated us. Then he changed the subject.

"Jon, I'm dying," he said. "I've got terminal cancer and I'm dying. I just wanted to let you know, because I don't want you to be like me. I want you to be with your kids. It's not all about football, breaking down film. Be with your family. Don't let this game consume you until it's over for you, like I let it do to me. There's more to life than this."

What Bobb told me made an impression. I always make a point to remind myself of my wife and kids. I don't know how long I'm going to coach, but right now it's all I want to do. At the same time, I'm aware of how precious life is and how vulnerable we all really are, even if we try to convince ourselves otherwise. To see someone physically deteriorate in front of your eyes—someone you always thought of as being so strong, so tough, so invincible—was horrible. Bobb's passing was a huge loss for me. There are times I think that every game I coach successfully is a testament to Bobb.

After Super Bowl XXXVII my mom got a phone call from Bobb's wife, Teckla. She didn't know how to reach me, so she called my mom to say, "I just think it's important that I let you know if Bobb were here today he would be calling to say how proud he was of Jon. I know he thought a lot of him. Bobb's only regret was that he never got to coach with Jon."

I could not think of a higher compliment.

# SEVEN

# When Opportunity Calls, You Answer on the First Ring

At Green Bay, I had my hands full coaching Sterling Sharpe (#84).
(Harmann Studios)

As THE 1990 SEASON wound down—with the 49ers headed to a third straight NFC Championship Game, which we would lose to the Giants on a last-second field goal—Mike Holmgren lined up an interview for me for an assistant coaching job on Paul Hackett's staff at the University of Pittsburgh. Paul had been the offensive coordinator of the 49ers before Mike, and they knew each other in coaching circles. Jerry Attaway, who was the 49ers' strength coach, had worked with Hackett, and Paul had asked Mike and Jerry to keep an eye out for someone who could help him work with quarterbacks while also being the receivers coach at Pitt.

My first reaction was that the 49ers were just looking to get rid of me—that after only one year I had overstayed my welcome in San Francisco. Mike assured me that that wasn't the case.

"Hey, look, you need to go coach," he said. "You're a young guy. You've learned a lot of football. You've got to go coach. And Paul Hackett's a guy that has a lot of theory that you believe in, that you've been trained to coach in."

Coach Holmgren said something else that really stuck with me: "If I ever do get a head coaching job, I'd feel better considering hiring you if you had some experience coaching as opposed to taking notes." If he would have told me to go to Binford Elementary School in Bloomington, Indiana, to coach quarterbacks, I would have done it, because I was going to do whatever Mike told me to do. I also knew that this was sound advice. As a young guy I had to take what I had learned and go apply it and see if I could get some results. You can only be a scribe for so long.

We were also talking about the Pitt Panthers. The list of players they had sent to the NFL was so impressive, it was hard to believe—Hugh Green, Rickey Jackson, Mark May, Dan Marino. That's a big-time football program. BIG TIME!

The interview with Coach Hackett was set up before our next-to-last game of the season, at home against New Orleans. The only problem was that Cindy Brooks, my wife-to-be, had flown in to visit me all the way from Atlanta—where she had moved after graduating from Tennessee to work as an assistant director of residents' life at Berry College. As soon as she arrived at my apartment, I had to tell her I was getting on a plane for Pittsburgh. Cindy was not happy.

By that time I had scraped together enough money to buy a car. It was an old white Delta 88 that the players called "Uncle Buck," because it looked like the big, beat-up bomb John Candy drove in that movie. As if I hadn't already done enough to put a strain on our relationship, I had Cindy drive me to the airport in "Uncle Buck."

I landed in Pittsburgh at about 6:30 P.M., checked into my hotel near the campus, and waited for a call from Coach Hackett, who was supposed to take me out to dinner that night. Finally, at about 10:30, the phone rang.

"Let's go out to dinner," Paul said.

Little did I know that I was dealing with a real late-night kind of guy, one of the all-time grinders in the history of the business. Paul and his wife, Elizabeth, picked me up and we ate at a nearby restaurant. When it got to be around midnight, I began to feel a little tired and a little concerned because we hadn't really talked much about football up to that point.

"Let's go back to my house," Paul said, looking fresh, like he was ready to start a new day. He has one of the greatest personalities I've ever been around. Always up. High energy. Positive. No fear. Elizabeth is the same way.

Paul had one of those old, huge homes with the classic architecture that you don't see much of anymore, right on campus. The university had thrown it in as a perk when he took the head coaching job. It must have had seventeen bedrooms and stood five stories tall. I mean, this place was so big, it needed elevators.

Inside this huge house was a huge office that had film projectors and grease boards, everything he needed to keep working after hours. Paul used it as his laboratory, which would serve as the blueprint of the laboratory that I would put in my house in Tampa many years later. That was where the interview would take place.

"So, Jon," Paul said, "what are you guys doing against two-deep?"

I was ready for that, because I had studied all of the 49ers' audibles for Cover Nine, which was how we referred to two-deep zone coverage: Jet Right T 15, 50 Bingo Pick, 20 Y. I went up to one of the grease boards and started drawing these plays. I could draw the fronts, the coverages, the progressions of the quarterback's reads. I was ready.

"Ho, ho, ho, ho," he said, stopping me in mid-diagram. "Tell me about the feet of the quarterback. Tell me about his footwork as he reads these plays."

I didn't know how to respond because, although I had looked at all of those audibles, I never learned them from the standpoint of the quarterback's technique. Just then it dawned me that I wasn't nearly as ready as I thought I was. I suddenly remembered what Joe Montana had told me about Coach Hackett before I left: "This guy knows what he's talking about. And the interview is going to be an attack. He's going to attack everything that you think you know, and you'd better be ready for any kind of question as it pertains to the quarterback. Any kind of question! If you think you love quarterback play, wait until you meet this guy."

I wasn't even close to ready. Coach Hackett went on to ask me even more basic questions that I couldn't answer, like exactly how a quarterback should take the snap from the center. And it made sense for him to want to find out how much I knew about these areas because I was being interviewed to coach quarterbacks, as well as receivers. I was supposed to be a guy who could technically teach an eighteen-year-old kid from Aliquippa, or wherever he was from, how to get underneath the center and then get away explosively. I had to be able to teach him about the simple acceptance of the snap, beginning with how far apart his feet were supposed to be. Are you going to have a heel-to-toe relationship? Are you going to be square in your footwork? Are you going to take a punch step and then reach, or are you just going to screw that left foot in and pivot off of it? I had never thought about those things. Being around Coach Hackett was like being around a walking, talking textbook on quarterback play.

What I had discovered during that interview was that I had learned a lot of good plays and a lot of good protections and a lot of good schemes, but I needed to become more technical as it pertained to the quarterback. I needed to learn more about the mechanics of quarterback play. I had been watching and listening to Mike Holmgren talk to Joe Montana and Steve Young about watching out for this blitz and that blitz, and I wasn't really thinking about the mechanical aspects of the job. Mike did have some daily footwork lessons, but it was nothing like what you would give some eighteen- or nineteen-year-old kid. And why would it be? He was working with two of the most talented quarterbacks in the history of the game. Plus maybe I was just so consumed with strategy that I had slighted myself by overlooking the fundamentals of the position.

Either way, I think Coach Hackett sensed that and he went in for the kill.

When I flew back from Pittsburgh I was convinced that I knew nothing about quarterbacks, that I was a total moron. But I couldn't have done too poorly, because he did tell me that I had the job. I couldn't wait to get back to tell Cindy the good news when she picked me up at the airport. I was ready to ask her to marry me because I had what I felt was my first legitimate, big-time coaching job. I had been a grunt at Tennessee, a grunt at Southeast Missouri State, a grunt at Pacific, a grunt at San Francisco. When I got the job at Pitt, I felt I could be a good husband. I could be a professional workingman. I was twenty-seven at the time, a few years sooner than I had planned to marry but close enough.

But when I landed, no one was at the airport to pick me up. I couldn't afford a telephone, so I had no way to check if Cindy was at my apartment. I just figured that she had left me. I could just hear her saying, "I've followed this guy to Southeast Missouri. I followed him to the University of the Pacific. Now we spend all the money that both of us have to fly me all the way out to San Francisco, and he can't even be here with me?" I didn't have any cash for a cab, but I did have a credit card, which I was able to use to rent a car and drive myself home. As soon as I walked in the door, I found Cindy crying. It turned out that "Uncle Buck" had broken down on her way to the airport. It was really cold, as it tends to get in San Francisco, and she had almost frozen to death trying to get back to my apartment. A day or so later, I drove her to a jeweler. I took almost all the money I had saved, about $1,200 or $1,300, and I got her a .45-carat marquis-shaped diamond ring in a nice little setting. Cindy wore that ring until after my final season as head coach of the Raiders, when I replaced it with a much bigger diamond.

When we got married that summer, Coach Hackett gave me $500 from his own checkbook for my honeymoon. That came in handy. We got a one-bedroom apartment in North Hills.

Thanks to Jerry Attaway, the 49ers' strength coach who helped hook me up at Pitt, Cindy got a job as a personal trainer for Nicki DeBartolo, the youngest daughter of Eddie DeBartolo, Jr., who lived in his hometown of Youngstown, Ohio. Two or three times a week Cindy would drive her old blue Subaru from Pittsburgh to Youngstown to train Nicki at the DeBartolo estate.

I wasn't looking for a relationship with a woman who necessarily had an interest in football. I wanted a different perspective. I didn't want her to call plays or help me study my game plan. I wanted to be with a woman who was sincere, who was an independent person—somebody who excited me and dazzled me. Somebody exactly like Cindy. When I'm with football, it's personal, it's what I do. When I get away from it, the last thing I would ever want to do is take my wife out to One Buc Place and start diagramming Double Switch Beaters, you know what I mean?

Cindy is off the charts as a wife and mom. The most satisfying thing for me is going to work knowing that my kids are taken care of. She doesn't have to be at every game or come with me every year to the owners' meetings. She stays at home with the kids. She makes an enormous sacrifice, very much like my mom did with my brothers and me. That, to me, is huge.

When I met Coach Hackett I was totally convinced that he could help me continue to learn, because he was another Bill Walsh coaching disciple. For a young coach, the next-best thing to getting to work directly with Bill Walsh was to work with the people who had been around him. I had been working with Mike Holmgren, who was with Bill up to the time of his retirement, so I got a sense of what he was like at the end of his coaching career. Bobb McKittrick had been Walsh's offensive line coach forever, so he gave me the historical perspective. Paul had been the 49ers' quarterbacks coach in Walsh's early San

Francisco years. That would give me three different interpretations of one of the greatest coaches in the history of the game.

Coach Hackett was there for "The Catch" by Dwight Clark from Joe Montana, to beat Dallas in the 1981 NFC Championship Game and put the 49ers in their first Super Bowl. He was with Tom Landry, who had handpicked him to be his offensive coordinator with the Cowboys. He was a superstar coach; he still is, as offensive coordinator for the New York Jets. Chad Pennington is a great quarterback for the Jets, but I also know that Paul has helped him tremendously.

The best part about the responsibility that Coach Hackett gave me with the quarterbacks at Pitt in '91 was that it was all carefully monitored, carefully scrutinized so that everything I did would truly be a learning process. Some of the greatest lessons came when Paul had me watch film and grade each play by the quarterback based on the footwork, the decision, and the location of the throw. I had to type up a detailed account of how I saw each play. There were no letter grades or numbers involved, just a thorough assessment that had to be in complete sentences and paragraphs.

A typical grade by me would read something like this: "This is a beautiful decision on 22 Z In. The primary receiver is open. Your rhythm is perfect. It's a five-step, one-hitch delivery. It's on time. The location of the throw is sensational. It's shoulder-high between the numbers, one he can catch easily." Or like this: "This one is a poor decision. Obviously, you've misread the coverage. They've rotated strong, which was not what we expected. However, your response is horrific. You're forcing the ball into a double zone and you failed to reset and locate your complementary receivers. To compound your error, you're late with the throw and it's thrown way behind the primary receiver. A catastrophe for the Pitt Panthers."

The grades, which covered about sixty-five plays, had to be written in such a way that the guy could replay the game in his mind ten or fifteen times. They weren't just items on a checklist where you just said, "Nice job" or "Good play." They had to be descriptive. They had to have depth. Before the quarterbacks could see them, however, I had to submit my assessments to Coach Hackett the Monday morning after a game. He would go over them like a professor grading a term paper. A lot of times when I got them back, they would be covered with red ink. He'd circle a bunch of plays and write, "See me in my office."

"I totally disagree with your evaluation of 76 X Shallow Cross," Paul would say. "The decision when the free safety rotates to the side of the motion is the exact correct one, indeed."

It wasn't really a two-sided conversation. If Coach Hackett wanted a grade changed, it was changed. I was on the money a fair amount of the time, but he wanted to have a discussion on just about every play. His main reason for doing that was to make sure the message he, as head coach, wanted to deliver was getting through to his quarterbacks. Coach Hackett also knew that each discussion would help provide me with the additional education I needed to develop as a coach.

For a young guy looking to coach quarterbacks, you couldn't have done much better than I did as far as being around the "H-men"—Harris, Holmgren, and Hackett. By the time I got to Pittsburgh I felt that I knew what I was talking about. I felt I could have conversations with guys I considered geniuses. I could talk with them about fronts, coverages, game planning, quarterback and receiver play, offensive line, protections. I could talk football all day and all night, whether I was working for a nighthawk like Paul Hackett or a morning person like Walt Harris. I was ready to roll.

We had some players at Pitt who would find plenty of NFL success: offensive guard Ruben Brown, center Jeff Christy and defensive lineman Keith Hamilton. Curtis Martin was a freshman running back. Our quarterback, Alex Van Pelt, was also a freshman. He would go on to break most of Dan Marino's school passing records, but we were a young team. We went 6–5 that season. We got off to a wonderful start, but then we kind of fell apart a little bit. We lost a heartbreaker to East Carolina; Jeff Blake beat us at the end of the game. We lost another heartbreaker to Penn State.

As I mentioned, I usually wake up at 3:17 A.M. Coach Hackett usually went to bed about that time. That made it a tough year for me physically because I'd start my day early and when I was kind of ready to wind down, Paul was just getting going. Whenever I see the movie *A Beautiful Mind*, I think of Paul Hackett. He's just like John Nash, staying awake day and night to come up with a brand-new football theory. I remember the week we were getting ready to play Notre Dame, he came up with a whole new package of plays, something he was convinced that the Fighting Irish had never seen or even thought of. We had changed some shifts and formations and I was thinking, *Man, we haven't really worked these plays very much*. But what Paul was doing was a classic Walsh-ism—hit the opposing defense with something it can't prepare for because it doesn't have any film of you running it.

"This offense is about plays that start off looking the same but are actually different," he would explain. "You want to present the illusion of sophistication and complexity, yet remain simple and basic."

We ended up getting our asses kicked by Notre Dame 42–7. Bill Walsh got his ass kicked sometimes as well. I still thought it was a hell of a plan. I felt pretty good about the element of surprise. I think our players believed in it, too, and it stimulated them. The changes weren't things our guys couldn't execute. It was just that we didn't block them that day and we turned the ball over and we didn't play good defense. Oh, and one more thing: Lou Holtz's Fighting Irish were rolling at that time.

It was just another reminder that even the greatest plans won't work if your players don't have what it takes to get the job done on a particular day. That's why I try not to be too deeply philosophical about this game. You're still talking about an eleven-man play—eleven men who've still got to do a job. Forget about the throw, the route, the catch, the decision, the feet and all that. If your left guard can't block their right defensive tackle at all, good luck, Sherlock.

When I started out in coaching my dad told me, "You don't want to be one of those guys who changes jobs every year just to change jobs. The only time you should change jobs is if you get a better job. When I left Dayton, I went to Indiana. When I left Indiana, I went to Notre Dame. When I got fired from Notre Dame, I went to the Tampa Bay Buccaneers. You don't want to go from UCLA to USC back to UCLA. You don't ever want to make lateral moves. You always want to get better."

He also stressed that it was more important to strive to be around blue-chip caliber people than at a specific school. Paul Hackett would be high on anyone's blue-chip coaching list.

Although this was the fourth college program I had worked for, my vision was totally on landing a coaching job in the NFL. I was hoping and praying every night that Mike Holmgren would get a head coaching job and maybe call me. At that time I did not want to recruit, which is a large part of what college coaches have to do. I did not want to spend half of my time calling recruits, going out with alumni, and checking on players' grades. I wanted to learn football and coach football. Still, I did work at being a good recruiter for Pacific and Pitt. I knew it was vital to our program, that it was every bit as important as coaching, maybe more important. But I did not like it at all. I didn't like flying all over the country, getting in a rent-a-car, driving to different high schools, calling recruiting coordinators, documenting my calls. I didn't learn one damn thing about football while doing that. I felt everybody else in coaching was blowing by me. Everybody else was getting better while I felt I was standing still.

The excitement I got from coaching at the college level was helping to get a play in the game plan and getting it called and seeing it work. It came from helping a young player develop, then watching him get into a game and do well. That was when I felt great. When I went to a high school and was able to get a player to sign a letter of intent, that wasn't as fulfilling at the time as maybe it should have been. That just never turned me on. Some guys are really geeked up to go recruiting. Maybe I will be, too, someday, but I'm not right now.

After the 1991 season ended at Pitt, the 49ers were knocked out of the playoffs despite finishing 10–6. But they still had one of the best offensive schemes in football, making Mike Holmgren a hot candidate for some head coaching jobs. I'd be watching TV at night and there would be all these stories about Mike interviewing in three or four places, including Minnesota and Green Bay.

As that was going on, we were having a month of recruiting weekends at Pitt, where we would bring in recruits and their parents for a basketball game, take them to dinner, and just do some general schmoozing. On one of those weekends I got home about eleven o'clock at night. Cindy was waiting up for me.

"Hey, Jon, you've got to call Mike Holmgren," she said. "He just called to say he got the Green Bay Packer job and wants you to call him right away. He's staying at the Embassy Suites in Green Bay. He's registered under an alias."

I dropped everything and called him up.

"I want you to come out here and work for me," Mike said.

I didn't know what the job was. I didn't even ask. All I knew was that it was a chance to get back in the NFL and to work with Mike again. I flew to Green Bay and signed a two-year contract.

It turned out that my role wouldn't be all that different than it was with the 49ers. I was sort of a glorified quality control guy. As Coach Holmgren pointed out, the duties didn't matter as much as the fact, at twenty-eight years old, I was working for the Green Bay Packers and he was going to put me in a position to get what I deserved—whatever that might be. To this day I believe that you get what you deserve in anything you do. If you do a poor job, you're going to get poor results. If you do a good job, you work your ass off, you've got a chance to have some success.

I also knew football and I was pretty sure that Coach Holmgren knew I knew football. Every once in a while as he was installing the offense with the other coaches he had brought in who weren't from San Francisco—Andy Reid (tight ends/assistant offensive line), Steve Mariucci (quarterbacks), Tom Lovat (offensive line) and Gil Haskell (running backs)—he'd check with me to confirm whether we were doing something we had done during my one season with the 49ers. That told me that a couple of years after that very first interview, he had developed some trust and respect for my understanding of his scheme. It was a satisfying feeling. I knew all those notes I had taken when I was around him and Bobb McKittrick would come in handy.

"Hey, Gruber, against this front did the center make a 'bang' call?" Mike asked.

"No, Bobb had him make a 'snuggle' call right there," I said. "He wouldn't commit himself to the full slide of the offensive line (to pick up a potential blitz off the edge). He would snuggle, he would stay inside and pop out late if that slot blitzer came." The expression on the faces of the some of the other coaches was like, "This guy might actually know what he's talking about."

On game day Mike called the plays and I was the one who signaled them to our quarterbacks, Don Majkowski and Brett Favre. This was before we had the communication system between the sideline and the quarterback's helmet. Mike would tell me the play through my headset, which also allowed me to hear his conversations with Steve Mariucci, who was in the press box.

Before games I would always go into Mike's locker and take a look at what he highlighted on his sideline sheet, how he prioritized the plays. I'd go, "Oh, he's going to be aggressive today, man." Then I'd tell the receivers, "Be ready. The ball's going to be coming to you guys all day."

Sometimes during a series I would write notes to Mike, just as I had with Walt Harris at Tennessee. I might just give him a reminder like, "You liked Fox 3 Naked Right Fullback Slide during the week. Don't forget that one." He might nod or he might say, "Get away from me." I'd pick my spots carefully. Remember, the guy stands six-five.

Green Bay gave me my first real exposure to front-office people because I wasn't included in a lot of the personnel meetings in San Francisco. And front-office people don't get any better than Ron Wolf, our general manager and one of the best personnel guys this game has ever seen. The first thing I noticed about Ron was that he was very thorough. He was on top of everything—college personnel, pro personnel and personnel that we had on Green Bay. He watched the practice film, as well as the game film. He gave all the coaches accountability and responsibility at our respective positions. We had to know who was in the draft, who was available in Plan B free agency at that time. We had to answer his questions in terms of how the players at our respective positions were performing.

Ron, who has since retired, has a commanding presence about him. When he walks into a conference room, it isn't a case where he feels the need to break the ice with a joke: "Did you hear the one about the guy who's walking down the street and his pants fall down?" Ron is all business all the time. He is not the kind of guy you go out and have a beer with. He is not the kind of guy you shoot the breeze with. He is an iceman and people respect the hell out of him. He gives you a sense of confidence that we have a plan.

When Ron asks you a question about a player, he doesn't want to hear some long, drawn-out explanation. I remember one day he asked, "Why isn't Robert Brooks starting, Jon?" I went on and on with my answer, which was exactly what he didn't want to hear. He just wanted the basic answers to basic questions. Why isn't he playing? How can he not play? When is he going to play? Do you know that? His meetings also were short and to the point. One time he began by saying, "We're going to trade for John Stephens," the running back we picked up from New England in 1993. "I think we can get this guy for a fourth-round pick. We're going to watch these three films on him. Mike, what do you think? Andy, what do you think? Steve? Gil? Jon?"

Ron was one of the most impressive guys I've been around in this business.

In 1992 we had two first-round draft choices. I was thinking that we were going to get some good players to turn around a team that had gone 4–12 and 6–10 the previous two seasons under Lindy Infante, who was a very a good offensive coach himself. I figured Ron would make two great picks, add some other good players through the rest of the draft and we'd be in business.

Then one day in February Mike came up to me and said, "Hey, Gruber, we just traded a first-round pick today for a player. I'm going to need you to go to the airport and pick him up."

"Who did we trade it for?" I asked.

"Brett Favre."

"Brett Favre? The guy from Southern Miss who was in Atlanta?"

"That's the one."

My first thought, which I kept to myself, was *Why would we give up a first-round pick for that guy?* The Falcons had made him a second-round pick the year before, but it wasn't as if he was being touted as a future All-Pro. Besides, we already had a good quarterback in Don Majkowski.

I drove to the airport to pick up Brett. I couldn't believe how loose—and I do mean l-o-o-o-s-e—he was for a young guy who had just been traded for a first-round pick. He felt no pressure, no responsibility. None. Zero. I think the first question he asked was "Do they have any fried okra around here?" I think the second thing he wanted to know was where he could get a beer.

Brett kept looking out the window like he had just been dropped off in the middle of Siberia. I didn't even think he knew he was playing for Green Bay. I thought he just felt lost. And all I could think was *What the hell were Wolf and Holmgren thinking?* I just didn't see how he was going to fit into our offense. He didn't seem detail-oriented or disciplined or meticulous or very eager to learn what we were doing. He wasn't the conformist that you'd maybe anticipate Mike Holmgren being interested in. He just didn't fit the mold. How in the hell is he going to call Red Left Switch Z Right Sprint Right GU Corner Halfback Flat? I got the impression that Brett wasn't all that concerned with such a challenge. Everything about his attitude said, "Just give me the ball and we're going to score."

The first time Brett walked in the office, he said, "How ya'll doin'?" You could almost hear everyone thinking, *We're going to build our franchise around this guy?* About four or five days later, Brett, wearing a hooded sweatshirt, did some throwing in the little dumpy bubble that served as the Packers' indoor practice facility before the beautiful Don Hutson Center was built. As Brett threw, I caught. How hard did he throw? Put it this way, a couple of times I swore he was going to make some new holes in me.

The next day Mike came up to me and said, "Hey, Gruber, what do you think about Favre?"

"I don't know," I said. "I'll say one thing, though. He can throw the shit out of the ball. He almost killed me yesterday."

We opened the season against Minnesota and got beat. We lost to Tampa Bay to go 0–2. In the third game we played against Cincinnati, and Don Majkowski hurt his ankle. He was on the ground for a long time. He could hardly walk. As I watched him struggling to leave the field, I thought, *Man, we're not going to win a game.*

Brett Favre took over. He barely knew the plays. He could hardly say the ones he did know. I wasn't sure if we knew what he was doing. Then he proceeded to make two or three throws that no one alive could make. We beat the Bengals on the last play of the game when Brett threw a bullet and hit Kitrick Taylor on a thirty-five-yard seam route for a touchdown with thirteen seconds left. That was the beginning of what we now know as one of the greatest quarterback stories in the history of the game.

Brett didn't get it done in Atlanta for whatever reason, but Ron Wolf saw that he was a prizefighter who, with training from some of the best quarterback coaches in the NFL, could become the heavyweight champion of the world. That's how I still look at Favre to this day. Whenever I see him I say, "Hey, there's the champ, man."

He has exceptional charisma with people. He is fun as hell to be around. He has the greatest physical, raw quarterbacking ability. He can run. He's tough. And did I mention he can throw the shit out of the ball?

My all-time favorite Brett Favre memory came in my third year in Green Bay, 1994, when we played Atlanta in the second-to-last game of the season and the final one ever in Milwaukee County Stadium before Lambeau would become the Packers' only home field. We needed to beat the Falcons to stay in the playoff hunt. It was third-and-goal. We had no time-outs left. We needed a touchdown to win the game. There were only about eighteen seconds left, time enough for two pass plays. "Whatever happens, don't scramble," Mike said after calling a couple of post routes. "Because we don't have any time-outs and if you get tackled in-bounds, the game's over. Throw it someplace where we have a chance to score or throw it away. *DO NOT* run around!"

Brett nodded like he understood. Then he started running around. He dived over the pylon to score a touchdown with fourteen seconds left to give us a 21–17 victory and set up our playoff-clinching win the following week over Tampa Bay. To me, in that Atlanta game, he just exploded onto the scene as one of the football's all-time competitors. I wish I had a dollar for every time Mike would say, "No! Noooo! Great throw! No! No! No! Yes! Good job, Brett! You're driving me crazy. I love ya, Brett, but you drive me crazy."

After my first year with the Packers, Paul Hackett became the offensive coordinator of the Kansas City Chiefs. He called Coach Holmgren to ask permission to interview me to become either the running backs coach or the receivers coach for the Chiefs. Since I was only handling offensive quality control in Green Bay, I saw it as a promotion. But under NFL rules at the time, an assistant coach under contract with one team could not go to another for a lateral position. You only could make an upward move to coordinator, assistant head coach and head coach. Mike didn't want me to leave. He refused to grant the Chiefs permission to interview me, then made me his receivers coach. I wasn't at all comfortable with the move, because Sherman Lewis, whom I had worked with in San Francisco, had coached receivers while also serving as Mike's offensive coordinator. Sherm knew his stuff as a receivers coach. Although he insisted to me that he was okay with being strictly a coordinator, I was very reluctant about taking the new job because I just wasn't sure if it really did sit well with Sherm.

But coaching the Packer receivers did give me the chance to work with the man I believe, to this day, is the greatest football player I've ever seen—Sterling Sharpe. If he hadn't suffered the neck injury that ended his career after the 1994 season, his seventh in the league, he might have approached Jerry Rice in some ways. Sterling had two of his best seasons when I was in Green Bay, catching 108 passes in 1992 and 112 in 1993, the year I became the receivers coach. His production had nothing to do with my coaching. It had everything to do with the fact he was just an exceptionally talented receiver.

Pound for pound, Sterling was the strongest man I've ever met. He was a beast, a mean, nasty, six-foot-one, 205-pound bitch of a football player. He could play any position on the field. Here was a guy who started at quarterback at South Carolina. He could throw a football eighty yards. He could play linebacker and knock your ass off. He could play strong safety. He probably could play tight end.

During period one of practice, when each position group was supposed to be doing its own individual drills, Sterling would actually run over with the linebackers and do a couple of minutes of work with them. He'd make contact with a blocker, then scrape, lock, lift and drive into another with a perfect form tackle. He'd run down to the defensive linemen, get in a stance, and hit the sled. He'd run over to the defensive backs and get in a couple of backpedals. He'd run over with the quarterbacks and throw a couple of balls. Then he'd come back to me and get the last thirty seconds of receiver drills.

Sterling played football the way Magic Johnson played basketball—always with a smile on his face. He had the loudest voice I've ever heard. It was like he had speakers in his shoulder pads. And he never stopped talking. Some of the coaches and other players might have found that irritating at times, but

Sterling was such a good player that they were all happy to have him on their side. Besides, how else was he supposed to prepare for his future gig with ESPN?

One of the things that made Sterling such a great receiver was that he never left his feet. He wouldn't jump up and cradle a ball and protect himself. He was going to stay on his feet, reach for that ball, expose his body, snatch the ball, bring it back down and explode on you. He had outstanding run-after-the-catch skills. He was always in a position to catch a ball and move the pile for yards or make a guy miss. He could make you miss or he could knock you out.

Sterling was tough as hell and a punishing blocker. As we were getting ready to play the Denver Broncos on *Sunday Night Football* in 1993, I made film cut-ups to show our receivers, when they had to block for the run, what they could expect from Dennis Smith, one of the hardest-hitting safeties in the league. "On all six- and eight-hole runs this week, we've got first force, as you know," I said. "Dennis Smith, number forty-nine, is going to fill the alley. As soon as he sees that tight end block, he sees the run action, he is filling the alley." I showed them what happened when J. J. Birden, a receiver for Kansas City, tried blocking for the run against the Broncos. Dennis Smith dropped a house on J. J. He went in there, filled the alley, knocked J. J. over, and held Marcus Allen to a one-yard gain.

"We've got to push that corner off," I said. "And when Dennis Smith forces, we've got to go get him. We've got to block the alley this week. He's filling it, man."

All of a sudden a very familiar booming voice filled the room.

"Nobody fills the alley against Sterling Sharpe!" Sterling said. "Nobody!"

"Dennis Smith's filling the alley, man," I said. "He fills the alley better than anybody in football."

The night of the game, we called 18 Bob, a running play. As Sterling broke from the huddle, he headed right toward our sideline. "Hey, Gru!" he yelled. "Watch this! Watch him fill the alley!"

After the snap, Smith came down toward the alley, but he kind of feathered a little bit. He didn't hit it the way he did against Birden. Sterling pushed off the corner, Ray Crockett, then he blocked Smith and we got about a four- or five-yard gain.

"Nobody fills the alley against Sterling Sharpe! Nobody!" Sterling said, just in case I didn't happen to notice. "He don't want me! You should have known, Gru! And in your tip sheet next week, remember: Nobody fills the alley against Sterling Sharpe!"

Sterling had a great feel for football. He knew where the zones were. If it was man-to-man, he knew when to turn it on and separate with his excellent acceleration. For a big guy, he had unusual flexibility; he could get in and out of cuts easily. And, man, was he physical against bump-and-run coverage.

His work ethic was unbelievable. On game day he had a ritual in which he had to catch something like eighty-four balls before every game. I know, because I was the one who had to throw them to him. High balls. Low balls. Side balls. Then I'd get about two feet away and shovel about seven or ten balls that he'd catch quickly. On a cold day—and we had a lot of those in Green Bay—I had to take my coat off to throw. I'd be freezing and there was Sterling, in a short-sleeved shirt with his socks rolled down to his ankles. His body would be covered in Vaseline to help keep him warm. He'd be catching and talking, catching and talking.

Coaching Sterling Sharpe was a real challenge. He'd let you coach him during the week, but on game day you couldn't coach him very much. As you might imagine, that could present some problems, such as when we played New England. Mike called 22 Z In, which Sterling caught for a nine-yard gain. That was three yards shorter than the route called for. Mike was pissed.

"How's it second-and-one on 22 Z In?" he yelled. "That's a twelve-yard cut. He's cutting his routes short. You'd better go get on his ass, Jon. Get on his ass! I'm watching you. Get on his ass!"

Knowing how tough it was to get after Sterling on game day, I had to think fast. I ran toward Sterling, waving my arms and looking agitated, but when I got close to him I never said a single word—I just moved my mouth so that Mike would think I was really letting him have it. I don't even know if Sterling knew I was there and I didn't care. I wasn't messing with him during a game, but I was doing what I had to do to satisfy Mike.

I can still hear him saying, "You have all week to get me ready. On game day, it's up to me to perform." I always thought that made perfect sense, which is why I take the same approach to this day. I tell our players, "Coaches get Wednesday, Thursday, Friday and a walk-through on Saturday. That's our time to help you guys get ready to play. Sunday's your day. We're going to make some adjustments, as you know, but we're not going to be telling you where to line up and where to go and what to do. That's your day to perform."

Coach Holmgren believed that when a receiver ran a slant pattern his split had to be two yards outside the numbers to give him some extra field to work with. Normally if you line up on the outside edge of the numbers as they are located on an NFL field, you're usually in pretty good shape to run any kind of inside or outside route. But when we ran a slant, an inside-breaking route, Mike wanted the guys to be a little wider in their splits, so we always referred to that as "plus two."

The receivers insisted on lining up closer to the numbers and Mike would get on my ass. "Their splits are too tight," he would say. "I don't like their splits."

So I'd go into our meetings and say, "Will you guys please take bigger splits?"

Sterling was the first to speak up on the subject. Naturally.

"I line up on the outside edge of the numbers on every play," Sterling said. "Runs, passes, inside routes, outside routes, I'm on the outside edge of the numbers. Period! That's what I do, that's my deal. I'm on the outside edge of the numbers. That way I have no split identification for me. I'm like a thief in the middle of the night. I don't give away nothing. I'm always on the outside edge of the numbers. Period!"

Another of our receivers with definite opinions about splits was Mark Clayton. He came to the Packers in '93, well after his highly productive seasons in Miami with Mark Duper and Dan Marino. I called him "The Riddler," like the character from Batman, because he had that same sick laugh.

"Hey, man, when I line up two yards outside the numbers, why don't I just give the corner a Hallmark greeting card and say, 'Hey, I'm runnin' an inside route'?" Mark said. "I ain't runnin' an outside route. I'm runnin' an inside route and the corner lines up inside, knowing I'm going in there.

"Now Don Shula wasn't a bad coach, either, man. Don Shula let me line up on the inside edge of the numbers and widen on my departure and then run the slant. When I line up on the inside edge of the numbers, the corner thought I was running an outside route and he lined up in an outside technique, so the slant worked better."

I was thinking, *That's a hell of a point.* Mark and Sterling both made valid points, but here I was with one receiver who wanted to line up on the outside edge of the numbers because he wanted to be a thief in the middle of the night, another guy who wanted to line up on the inside edge because that was how he was trained by the winningest coach in NFL history, and a head coach who wanted all the receivers to line up two yards outside of the numbers.

Robert Brooks? He'd line up six yards outside the numbers if you wanted him to. He'd line up on the sidelines. All the young guys—Ron Lewis, Terry Mickens, Bill Schroeder—would line up wherever you told them to as well. Sharpe and Clayton were doing it their way. In fact, the first time a slant route was called in practice after they spoke up about their splits, Clayton lined up on the inside edge of the numbers. The cornerbacks saw this and started talking to the safety, "Watch the under! Watch the under!" They were looking for a shallow cross or some kind of inside route. Clayton ran his wide departure slant, and of course he was wide open.

Not that that mattered to Mike.

"These splits are killing me!" he yelled. "I don't want them on the inside edge! I asked for your guys to be at a plus two, and now we've got one on the inside edge! Who's coaching who here?"

Finally the receivers felt the wrath I was getting because of their refusal to take bigger splits. Did that make them come around immediately? Let's put it this way, in 1994, my last season in Green Bay, the receiver splits were a lot wider than they were my first year there.

In 1993 the Packers had targeted two blue-chip free agents to sign—Reggie White, the dominant defensive end for the Eagles, and Harry Galbreath, an offensive guard with the Dolphins. Both guys had played at Tennessee, although only Harry and I were there at the same time. When we were talking about how much we wanted Galbreath during a meeting, I told Ron Wolf, "I know Harry Galbreath. I used to live right next door to him in the Stokley Athletic Center. He and Bruce Wilkerson were my next-door neighbors."

"Yeah, right," Ron said.

When Galbreath's name came up a second time I again said, "I know this guy."

The next thing I knew, I was on a plane to Clarksville, Tennessee. I was on a mission to recruit Harry. I spent a couple of nights at his house and told him all about the high quality situation he would be coming into with the Packers. It wasn't as easy a sell as I thought it would be.

"Hey, Gru, Green Bay's cold, man," Harry said. "It's really cold. I can't play in the cold."

One night we played pool and I issued Harry a challenge. "If I beat you at your house, on your table, you've got to come to Green Bay," I said. I won, in a stunning upset. We ended up signing Harry, as well as Reggie. Did my clutch pool playing have anything to do with us getting Harry? I'll always believe it did.

Getting Reggie was supposed to turn us into a Super Bowl team. Somewhere along the line, we forgot we actually had to earn that status on the field. The result was that we started the '93 season 1–3. We weren't playing well at all. Reggie called a team meeting. It was supposed to be players only, but I couldn't help but kind of eavesdrop on it, because I knew my man Sterling was going to have something to say.

"We've all got to step up individually," Reggie said to the rest of the players. "We've got to dig down deep now. We've got to make plays."

"Hey!" Sterling said, in that booming voice. "You've got to make plays. I've got to make plays. We're the highest-paid guys on this football team. How many sacks do you have in the first four games?"

Sterling called Reggie out. It got heated a little bit with stuff being said back and forth. The next game was that Sunday night game against Denver. Reggie put that legendary hump move on the Broncos a couple of times where he would get that low center of gravity and great leverage, maneuver his hand underneath the offensive tackle's armpit and use the guy's own weight to literally lift him off the ground and throw him upfield. Sterling did his part and we ended up winning 30–27. We went on to win three in a row, finishing 9–7 and going to the playoffs.

I'll never forget that meeting. What I learned was that, although they might not always admit as much publicly, the highest-paid players—the guys who are making all the money, no matter how they got there or whether they're in their first year, third year or eighth year—have a feeling of accountability deep down inside. And they should. They have to play at a higher level than everyone else. That's exactly why they do get all that money.

A year later we were playing the Los Angeles Rams. Late in the game Jackie Slater, the Rams' veteran tackle and future Hall-of-Famer, got hurt, and Wayne Gandy, a rookie from Auburn, took his place. Gandy lined up on the side Reggie wasn't. But right before the snap Reggie ran over to our other end, Matt Brock, and threw him on the other side, because Reggie wanted to rush Gandy. And just as you would expect from a matchup between the NFL's all-time sack leader and a rookie, Reggie just blew right past him and sacked Chris Miller to help us to a 24–17 win.

For the second year in a row, we opened the playoffs with a four-point win over the Detroit Lions in the wild-card round, only to turn around the following week and get bounced out in Dallas. Still, you just knew that you were on the ground floor of something special, that Mike Holmgren and Ron Wolf were putting together all the pieces for a Super Bowl run. To be around all that talent was amazing. Even more amazing was the talent that no one even knew we had at the time. In 1993 we used a fifth-round draft pick on a quarterback named Mark Brunell, who never took a snap for us and didn't make a name for himself until after Ron traded him to Jacksonville two years later for third- and fifth-round picks. In 1994 we signed an undrafted free agent named Kurt Warner, who also never took a snap in Green Bay and was cut before his rookie season even began. You probably know him better now as the two-time NFL MVP quarterback of the St. Louis Rams.

The only time I actually noticed Kurt in his only training camp with the Packers was when he threw to the receivers I coached during our individual period. I didn't exactly pay a whole lot of attention to his passing ability. He would just step and throw. You told him what to do, where to go, when to be there, and he just carried out every assignment. Otherwise, he was obscure. I don't believe a lot of guys ever met Kurt, ever even knew his name. He didn't say much at all. He was a really shy guy. He was maybe a little bit intimidated by being in the NFL.

Besides Brett, the other quarterbacks in camp were Brunell and Ty Detmer, leaving Kurt to get about three reps in practice. I remember Steve Mariucci telling a story that one day when it was Kurt's turn to get under center he said, "That's all right. Give my reps to Ty." Maybe at that point the whole experience was just overwhelming to him, which is just unbelievable when you think about all that he has accomplished since.

I still give Steve and Mike a hard time about not recognizing great talent that was right under their noses. I'll say, "You know, I saw him every day. He was throwing ball drills to my receivers. I could have told you he was a great player, but you didn't listen." Of course they could say the exact same thing to me. None of us saw the talent Kurt had.

Every once in a while just for fun I'll watch a VCR tape of the 1996 Arena League championship between the Tampa Bay Storm and the Iowa Barnstormers. Right there, for all the world to see, is Jay Gruden out-dueling Kurt Warner to lead the Storm to a 42–38 victory against the Barnstormers. Every time I see it I get goose bumps.

After 1994 season, the 49ers, with Steve Young leading the way, beat San Diego in the Super Bowl. They just ripped them. That win allowed Steve to finally climb out of Joe Montana's shadow and be recognized as the topflight quarterback he was. It also gave Mike Shanahan, who had been the 49ers' offensive coordinator, the chance to become head coach in Denver.

Not long after that, Coach Holmgren called me into his office. When you're built like the Abominable Snowman, you need a lot of space to work, which was exactly what Mike had—a giant office with a giant desk and a giant wooden door. After I walked in, Mike, while sitting behind his giant desk, picked up one of those remote garage door openers, pressed the button, and that giant wooden door swung shut. I had never seen anything like that before. The door just closed on his command.

"Hey, I just wanted you to know that Carmen Policy [then 49ers' president] called," Mike said. "He wanted permission to talk to you about becoming the 49ers' quarterbacks coach."

"That's great," I said. "That is awesome."

I saw it as an incredible opportunity because at the time, Steve Young was at the very top of his game. He was the Michael Jordan of football. He was the man. But Mike ended that conversation fast.

"I'm not going to let you go," he said.

"But it's a chance to work with Steve Young."

"Why would I let you go to San Francisco? We're trying to beat them. They're in the NFC. We're in the NFC. I'm not letting you go."

Mike knew I loved him and that I would do whatever he said. I still would do whatever Mike said because of loyalty and because of what he did for me. I was torn because San Francisco still was the mecca of football, but it meant a lot that Mike thought that much of me to tell me that he was keeping me there.

About an hour after I left Mike's office he called me back in. He used that garage door opener again. Only this time he seemed a little upset. Ray Rhodes, who had been Mike's defensive coordinator for our first two years in Green Bay before returning to San Francisco in the same capacity, had just taken the head coaching job in Philadelphia. He also had just called Mike to ask to talk to me about being his offensive coordinator.

I was no different from any young player or young coach. I wanted to go, man. I wanted to do more than I was doing. I needed to find out if I was any good. I needed to find out if all those notes I had taken, if all that work I had done was worth it. I had to go and put my ass on the coals, man. I had to see if I could do this.

Mike understood my ambition. Plus this was an opportunity I knew I wasn't going to get any time soon with the Packers. They had Sherman Lewis. They had a talented quarterbacks coach in Steve Mariucci. They had another up-and-coming guy in Andy Reid. They had an accomplished running backs coach in Gil Haskell, who would go on to become offensive coordinator in Carolina and Seattle. They had Tom Lovat, one of the top long-standing offensive line coaches in football history.

I had coached tight ends and wide receivers. I had listened to top line coaches in Tom and Bobb McKittrick. This was an opportunity for me to become a coordinator and get back to the quarterback. I needed to get back to the quarterback. It all went back to my dad, who said that I had to coach the quarterback, I had to learn how to talk to the quarterback, I had to be responsible for what the quarterback did.

You can go to medical school and train to become a doctor, like my brother Jim did. You can listen to lectures and take notes and watch surgeries, but at some point you've got to take that scalpel and you've got to do the incision. A lawyer's got to try his first case; he can't just read law books his whole life. I was no different from those people or a quarterback getting to face an NFL defense for the first time. You can only sit in meetings and go to minicamps and training camps for so long. At some point you've got to go out there and do it.

The way I understood this business, opportunities like this rarely knock. When you hear the knock, you've got to open the door. By God, I was going to seize the moment and never look back.

# EIGHT

# "Boy Wonder or Boy Blunder?"

## Randall, Watters, Cats, Rats and Eagles

Ready for game day as offensive coordinator of
the Eagles. (Ed Mahan/Philadelphia Eagles)

"**P**HILADELPHIA? YOU'LL GET EATEN ALIVE in Philadelphia. The media. The fans. The scrutiny. It's a tough place to play. It's a tougher place to coach."

That was what people kept telling me when, at the tender age of thirty-one, I became the NFL's youngest offensive coordinator in 1995. Not "Way to go, Jon!" Not "This is a great opportunity, Jon!" Basically the message I got was that I was about to become just another helping of food for a town that can never get its fill of letting its sports teams know when they aren't getting the job done.

The Eagles were coming off a really bad year, starting 7–2 and losing every one of their last seven games. Their quarterback, Randall Cunningham, had had a rough season. They were cutting loose William "The Refrigerator" Perry, the big defensive tackle who wasn't the same player he had been for the Bears' Super Bowl team, and Herschel Walker, the great running back who also was on the downside of his career. They were in a contract dispute with cornerback Eric Allen that was not going to be resolved. And they had a new owner, Jeffrey Lurie, trying to clean up a pretty big mess.

I suppose all those issues and all the warnings I had received were what woke me up in the middle of my first night in town. For a second I had no idea where I was. Then I realized I was at the Philadelphia Airport Holiday Inn. I thought, *Holy cow! What did I just do?*

Those thoughts only intensified the first time I saw Veterans

Stadium. I kept looking for a sign that said, CONDEMNED! but at the time this was home sweet home for the Eagles. It wasn't just that the Vet was old and run down. It was that we had to work underground. Our offices, our locker room, our weight room, all our facilities were literally underneath this dump of a structure.

As usual I got up early in the morning and drove in the dark to my first day at work. As I pulled into the staff parking lot I noticed there were cats all over the place. I'm not talking one or two cats. I saw maybe twenty or twenty-five cats at four o'clock in the morning. They were big cats and they were everywhere. I saw them when I was jogging around the stadium at lunch. I saw them when I went home at night.

The next day I came to work I saw all those cats again. I saw them the next day and the day after that. There was a security guard, an old Philly guy, who worked on the upper level where we parked. Finally, by about the fourth day I showed up for work, I asked him, "What's with all the cats?"

"You want cats or rats?" he said. "The cats eat the rats."

"I gotcha man," I said. "I'd rather have cats."

One of the first things I do after getting to the office is grab myself a cup of coffee. Even that was an adventure at the Vet. There were no automatic drip coffeemakers, just the old-fashioned kind where you'd press a button and it would make the sickest sound, like someone moaning with pain. Grinds would come out of the spout, squishing together into what looked like a cup of mud.

I was confident we could overcome the rats, cats, and everything else that made that stadium a house of horrors for anyone who had to spend more than five minutes there each day. I was confident we could succeed because we had Ray. He was a big-time guy, a very marketable guy. The 49ers had just won the Super Bowl and Ray had been their defensive coordinator. Every newspaper had a quote from someone saying that he was going to do a hell of a job as a head coach. I knew Ray's capabilities. I had sat in his DB meetings in San Francisco. I had watched the great things he had done as defensive coordinator with the Packers.

Ray had an unbelievable charisma about him. He had a great way of delivering his plan to the players so that they believed it was going to work and left the meeting room saying, "We're going to kick some ass!" And why wouldn't they believe? A lot of the theory Ray brought with him came from San Francisco, where he had worked with a truly great defensive coach in George Seifert. They had multiple fronts and coverages. They created the "elephant" position where defensive end Charles Haley could rush the passer while taking advantage of a mismatch against a back trying to block him. Good luck. Or Charles could drop in space and cover a back or cover a zone. It was a unique concept back then, although Ray was good enough to adjust with the times and generate new ideas.

I had known all along what Ray expected me to do, which was help him implement a program modeled after the one we saw the 49ers use when we were together in San Francisco. A lot of it wasn't about X's and O's. It was more about philosophy. We were going to take advantage of the notes that I had made about everything from setting up an offseason program and training camp to the player profiles we were looking for, which remain the same to this day. We wanted big receivers who give you yards after the catch; versatile tight ends who can run downfield, catch the ball and block; fullbacks who aren't just road graters, but guys who have some subtleties, who can catch the ball, who can run patterns and who understand protection; halfbacks who can line up in any eligible position, run patterns, catch the hell out of the football and run from every spot in the backfield—I-formation, split backs, off-set backs; offensive linemen who can pull, trap and run. We wanted reliable, heady players. Above all, we wanted people who loved football.

It wasn't just a case of Ray having a certain way he wanted

things done and trying to convince everyone else to believe in it. In me he had another guy with the same philosophy, and together we would try to sell it to everybody else in the organization—the personnel people, the owner and so forth.

At the time, the coaching staff consisted of exactly two people—Ray and yours truly. Assembling the rest of the staff wasn't going to be easy, because this was a team that been struggling, and there weren't a lot of guys available Ray had ever worked with, because they were under contract with other teams. Ray allowed me to help him in the hiring process, although he obviously would have final say on all hires. My top priority was to find a quality offensive-line coach, someone who could do the things I had seen Bobb McKittrick do as far as getting five guys to block just about any play you needed them to block, because that's what ultimately determines whether the game plan you spend all that time putting together is worth the paper it's printed on. I needed somebody who would work with me and who had a common philosophy to go where we wanted to go.

We interviewed a lot of college guys and pro guys. The more people we interviewed, the more obvious it became that I probably was going to have to find someone from the college ranks. One of the best sources I had in my search was my dad, who besides being a college scout and an ex-coach is a pretty astute guy who appreciates good, solid, on-the-field coaching. One day I asked him, "Who's the best college line coach you've seen all year?"

"I'll tell you, that guy at Wisconsin is a hell of a coach," my dad said.

"That guy" was Bill Callahan. I was aware of the work he was doing because when you're in Green Bay you can't help but follow the Badgers. I also got to know him when he and the rest of Barry Alvarez's staff would visit us in Green Bay during training camp as well as in April and May to observe what we were doing. It's common for NFL teams to invite college coaches to watch their practices and look at film so that they can pick up ideas that might be useful to them.

Bill never really hung out with anybody during those visits. He would just find a place where he could go and watch some tape. I was kind of a recluse myself, so I'd go sit with Bill and we would watch tape together. I got to know him a little bit and I liked the guy. When our search began, the Badgers had just beaten UCLA in the Rose Bowl, which made them the hottest program in the country and put their coaches in high demand. They had done a hell of a job.

I called Bill to come to Philadelphia for an interview. He made a great impression on Ray and all the other people in the organization who talked with him. We offered him the job, but the amount of money we were going to pay him was less than he was making at Wisconsin. I think everybody had assumed that he was going to take whatever we offered just to get in the NFL, but Bill had a hell of a life in Madison. He was a hotshot guy, especially after that Rose Bowl win. That's big in Wisconsin. We upped the ante and I gave him my best recruiting pitch.

"What are you guys going to do as an encore, man?" I asked him. "How about coming out here and helping us beat Dallas?"

Bill took the job. Other than working with Ray, that was probably the best thing that happened to me at Philadelphia. Bill had the same work ethic I did, if not a better one, and he stimulated me to push myself even more than I had up to that point. We had a lot in common, including the fact that we both were former Division III college quarterbacks. Bill did better at Illinois Benedictine College than I had done at Dayton, starting for three years and becoming an honorable mention All-America pick. But we still looked at ourselves as a couple of ham-and-eggers working together to try to get the Eagles' offense moving in the right direction.

•

I was brought to Philadelphia to help resurrect Randall Cunningham, who had once been the MVP of the league but had fallen on hard times. He had never worked in the "West Coast" offense before, but I believed he would be able to pick it up. After all, in Green Bay, Brett Favre, even when he was learning the system on the run, was enjoying magnificent success. As I watched Brett I thought, *Even though it might not be perfect, if you have a guy with superb ability—with a gun for an arm, great toughness, mobility—and a system like that, you could get results. That's how good this system is.*

Randall was a tremendous talent in his own right. He was "Robo-quarterback." He was "Starship Twelve." He was THE man at one time, one of the most feared men in football. When I was with the Packers he came to Green Bay, to Lambeau, and ripped us when Ray was our defensive coordinator. Randall could throw the ball the length of the field. He could punt. His hands were the size of frying pans. I've never seen a spiral like the one he threw.

About three weeks after being hired I got on an airplane and flew to Las Vegas, where Randall and his wife had a beautiful home. I called to let him know I was coming, but we had never met before, and when Randall opened the door he looked at me like I was the pool guy or someone who was there to clean his house.

"I'm Jon Gruden," I said.

Randall started laughing.

"You've got to be kiddin' me, bro," he said. "You've got to be kiddin' me, man."

I was supposed to help him regain his rhythm, his style, his status. To do that, I had to sell our system to him. First, though, I had to sell myself—that is, once Randall finally stopped laughing. He had worked with veteran coaches his whole career. He had been around big-time guys like Doug Scovil and Ted Marchibroda. Now here was little Jonny coming along to help him. Until I proved otherwise I don't think he believed I was qualified to do much more than hand him a towel and maybe a cup of water. It's different from the college game where kids the same age are always coming through. As young as I was then, I was sometimes dealing with veterans who were older than me and skeptical. But I knew if they just gave me a chance, I could do a good job. I was confident.

I brought along some game film for Randall and me to watch in the movie theater in his house. I had cut-ups from the 49ers and Green Bay. I had intercut some of the film to show a pass play we were going to be installing executed by both Joe Montana and Brett Favre. We talked about formations and how our terminology worked. He seemed to be listening and, more than anything, seeing if I knew what I was talking about. He was getting a feel for me as a person and for how to communicate with me so I could best understand him.

After a day of watching film Randall took me out to dinner at Caesar's Palace. He showed me a good time. He bought me an expensive shirt. He let me spend the night at his house. He gave me a feeling of acceptance. Randall knew that we needed to work together and trust each other.

"We can do this," I told him. "We really can do this if we work together. There are going to be some tough times and there are going to be some good times, but we've got to keep it on an even keel. We've got to relentlessly devote one year of our lives to get this 'Starship Twelve' going again. It's system. It's discipline. It's trust. It's commitment. It's a relationship we've got to work at."

When you're the starting quarterback in Philadelphia you're an important guy, right up there with the mayor. You're also exposed to as much criticism as praise, and probably a lot more criticism. But until that trip I didn't realize what Randall had been through during those previous ten years in Philadelphia as a black quarterback in the league, as a guy who had gone from enjoying unbelievable success to a guy who had endured some really trying times. I wasn't there for any of that. Randall had survived and maintained his status under Buddy Ryan, Richey Kotite, different quarterback coaches, different centers, different personnel changes.

He had a warning for me.

"Hey, bro, this place is going to change you," Randall said. "This place is tough. I just hope that you don't change, but just watch. They're going to try and split us apart. They're going to try and break you down. They're going to test you."

Who are "they"? "They" are the fans, "they" are the media, "they" are the people who have been testing coaches and players in Philly for years. I smiled at Randall.

"Well, bring it on," I said. "We're going to fight through this."

At the time, the fans and media were split on Randall. On one hand he had a devoted following, and on the other he had people who wanted him out of there, people who wanted a change. When you said something positive about Randall in the media you always had people there who were trying to say, "This guy's nuts thinking Randall Cunningham is going to be a positive player for this team."

My mission was to make Randall and the other quarterbacks as good as they could be. I reached back to everything I had ever learned about coaching the position, right down to soaking footballs with water so the quarterbacks could get used to handling a wet ball on snaps, handoffs and throws, because you never know what kind of weather conditions you're going to encounter during a game. I learned that from Walt Harris at Tennessee. We would actually have a big bucket of water on the practice field to dip the balls in during drills.

When they announced the starting offense for the first preseason game that year against Atlanta, Randall was, as usual, the last guy introduced. It was like Muhammad Ali being introduced for a fight. You had thirty-five or forty thousand fans cheering emotionally. You had twenty-five or thirty thousand fans who didn't want you to win, who were obviously against him.

By end of that game everyone was a Randall Cunningham fan because he completed twelve of fifteen passes and had a thirty-eight-yard run. He looked sharp. We won the game 25–17, and all you read and heard around town was how amazing our offense looked. This was only the preseason, but we might as well have just won the Super Bowl. I was "Boy Wonder" in the newspapers. We finished the preseason 4–0. We scored thirty-five points against New England. Our offense was rolling.

One of the best parts about my Philadelphia experience was that Ray Rhodes trusted me with the offense. He would come into offensive meetings and we would work together on the game plan, but he pretty much put the offense in the hands of the offensive staff. With that responsibility came a whole lot of pressure. Ray was a demanding guy. He expected the offense to have good execution, to be productive and to be balanced. In practice, defensive coordinator Emmitt Thomas and his staff would give us the proper motivation by challenging us in every aspect of offensive football.

Our chances of meeting Ray's expectations improved considerably the day we got Ricky Watters, the prized free-agent acquisition of 1995, from San Francisco. He had joined the 49ers in 1991, a year after I left. Ricky wasn't just a top-notch running back; he was a top notch football player—a complete player. We tried every which way but loose to get him the ball— throwing it to him, handing it to him. We just figured that whenever we got the ball in Ricky's hands, good things would happen.

Our first regular season game was at home against Tampa

Bay. As I ate breakfast that morning I saw a picture of myself in the paper, right on the front of the sports section, with a headline that said something like, "Boy Wonder and Starship Twelve." If I had any reason to feel good about myself, it was long gone by the end of the day, because we went out there and got our asses kicked 21–6.

That was the score when we had a first down at our own thirty-four-yard line with a little more than three minutes left. We tried to get the ball to Watters down the middle against their two-deep on a play we called 22 Strike. With Charles Dimry closing in, Ricky short-armed it. After the game Ricky told reporters, "I'm not going to jump up there and get knocked out. For who? For what? There's other days. I'm going to make a lot of plays."

In a matter of hours I went from "Boy Wonder" to "Boy Blunder," Ricky became "Mr. For Who? For What?" and as far as all the media and fans were concerned, Randall couldn't play in our offense. We were all on our way out—after one game.

Driving to work from my home in South Jersey, I'd hand my $2 to the guy in the tollbooth on the Walt Whitman Bridge and I'd hear, "Dumb ass! Bozo!" They didn't have a hard time spotting who I was because there aren't a lot of blond-haired, blue-eyed guys with freckles in Philly. I was getting killed. I felt I had let Ray down. I felt I had let everyone in the Eagles' organization down. I began to think that I should have stayed in Green Bay.

The following week we had to go to Arizona to face the Cardinals, who were coached by none other than Buddy Ryan. Buddy had taken the job a year earlier, and after going 1–1 against the Eagles he couldn't wait for another crack at his former team. The Cardinals were a bitch on defense, with blitzes from Clearwater Beach to the North Pole. They were going to be coming from everywhere.

We started out playing poorly in that game as well. Randall didn't have any rhythm. The timing of his throws was either late or early. He just wasn't right. We pulled him for Rodney Peete. Rodney had a great game and we won 31–19. We just connected from the moment he went in there. I'd call the play from the press box, such as "374 Omaha," and boom, he'd make the three-step drop and throw the quick out. He knew where to go against the blitz, throwing to the "hot" receiver, or he'd make an audible to the right play. He played his ass off and we were 1–1. Flying home from that game I had one of the best feelings of my life. It was my first win as an offensive coordinator, the first time as a coach where I felt I had really made a significant contribution to our team's success.

After working from the sideline through the preseason and in our opener I moved up to the press box for our second game. Actually Ray sentenced me to the box, and that was where I remained for the rest of my time in Philadelphia. When I became a head coach I went back to calling plays myself from the sideline. NFL rules allow only one coach on the sideline to talk to the quarterback on the field through the headset-to-helmet communication system, which means if you're calling plays from the box, you're giving it to another coach, who in turn is repeating it to the quarterback. By the time the quarterback gets the play, it's really second- or thirdhand information, depending on how you look at it. With me being connected directly to the quarterback, I can give Brad Johnson the play quicker, the offense can get in and out of the huddle faster and the tempo is better.

One of my big deals is tempo. I like the presentation. I like the flow of the game. I like the fact that we're always attacking, on offense as well as on defense. Another advantage to my talking directly to the quarterback is that I can give him a heads-up or a reminder about something, kind of coach him up a little bit. I really felt I could help Randall tremendously by giving him the play directly. I felt I knew what he needed because I had been with him all the time during the week. So when I gave him "Blue Right Y Motion 2 Jet Flanker Drive," I could add, "Don't forget the flanker's hot versus blitz. And use a hard count here; they'll jump offside when you're using motion." Or I might say, "Okay, you're in short yardage now, it's third-and-one. Green Right Close 14 Blast. If you don't like what you see, throw it away because I'm going to go for it on fourth down."

Well, we got the crap kicked out of us by the Bucs, and none of those great coaching points was worth a damn. After a while it became "Hey, let's try this . . ." Maybe I wasn't as ready as I thought I was to deal with having our players, coaches and fans—not to mention players from the other team—yelling at me the whole game as I tried to concentrate on calling the plays: "You're a dork! Give me the ball! What the hell are you doing?"

When it was over, Ray said, "You're going up in the box, man." I think he felt there would be less distraction by having me upstairs and Bill Callahan down on the field calling plays together while our receivers coach at the time, Gerald Carr, would relay them to the quarterback. Later on we hired Sean Payton to be our quarterbacks coach and I would send plays down to him on the sideline. I used to kill him. I'd say, "This is Double Wing Right F Short 72 Zebra Bingo Y Corner. Tell him the flanker's hot and don't forget 358 as an audible. Did you tell him? Did you tell him?"

The fact is, you are in a better position to call a game while sitting inside a closed-in booth. It's quiet. It's a better view. You get instant photographs taken right before the snap and right after the snap, from the sideline and end zone, that you can look at between series. It's really more conducive to calling a game if that's your job.

Trying to call the game from the field is hard, but nothing is harder than being hooked up to me on the headset when you're in the press box and I'm on the field because I'm an asshole. I'll call you every name in the book if I'm not getting the right answers to the questions I'm asking, or if the answers aren't coming fast enough. I've been wired and I've listened to myself talking to people, and I'm surprised somebody hasn't taken me out by now. I can't see from down there so when we hand the ball off I'm yelling, "What's the front? What the bleep happened, man? Did we run it at the three technique? Did we run it to the bubble [the uncovered area between the center and the tackle]? Who missed the bleeping block? Was it the right tackle? Damn it! What do you mean, you don't know? Do you guys know what the hell you're doing?" I'm brutal. I'm horrible.

We went back to Randall the following week against San Diego at home. Although he threw three touchdown passes, we lost 27–21. Even with the touchdowns Randall didn't play very well in that game, either.

As I walked over to practice one day that week I spotted a big white Lincoln Continental parked, its dark windows rolled up. All of a sudden the driver side window rolled down and I heard, "Hey, Jonny!" I looked inside at this smiling face and squinting eyes. It was Dick Vermeil, the legendary former coach of the Eagles. At the time, Dick was broadcasting college games for ABC. I had never met him before, but apparently he had been following what I was doing for the Eagles, and just out of the kindness of his heart he stopped by to console me a little bit over the fact we were struggling. He offered me a ride to practice, and I couldn't say yes fast enough.

Coach Vermeil's message to me was "Don't try so hard. You're doing a great job. Just don't try so hard. Go home, kiss your kids, kiss your wife. Don't go crazy." I nodded, but all I could think was *You're legendary for being Joe Workaholic.* This was a guy who two years after losing the Super Bowl with the Eagles left coaching because of "burnout," then came back fifteen years later with the St. Louis Rams and won the Super Bowl, then retired a second time after the '99 season, only to come back to coach again in 2001 with the Kansas City Chiefs.

But his stopping by that day meant a lot to me. He didn't have to do anything, and he gave me something I needed to hear at the absolute right time.

We would speak on a fairly regular basis after that. Every now and then, after a game he'd leave me a phone message that would say, "Hey, Jon, this is Dick Vermeil. I just wanted to tell you that you had a great balance between the run and the pass. Your mixture of plays was outstanding. Keep it up." You talk about somebody giving you some juice. Dick helped me tremendously in Philadelphia. To this day he is still one of my gurus, someone I can talk to on the phone at any time for advice. I love that guy.

In week four, Randall got us out to a 17–0 lead at Oakland, then the Raiders scored forty-eight consecutive points to drill us 48–7. I got together with Ray and we decided to make Rodney Peete the starter for our fifth game, in New Orleans. I called Randall into my office to break the news. To take away the starting quarterback job from someone who had held that position for ten years, who was a dynamic guy you knew could eventually run the offense the way it was supposed to be run, was terrible. It was horrible. It was awful. I felt I had let Randall down, but we were 1–3 and had to get some results. We had to get some better feedback on film that the quarterback was getting a feel for what we were doing. Plus the rest of the players had kind of migrated toward Rodney. They had seen him go into Arizona and play well and win. They were thinking, *Why don't we play Rodney?*

Rodney Peete had a strong vibe and a lot of charisma. When we announced that he was going to be the starter for our fourth game, against New Orleans, the whole team just swelled up. Everybody rolled up his fists and started fighting. By God, we ended up winning four in a row. We finished the season 10–6. We made the playoffs. We beat Detroit 58–37 in a wild-card game before losing in Dallas the following week. And Ray Rhodes was Coach of the Year.

Naturally Randall felt I had betrayed him.

"I told you this town would change you," he said. "I told you they'd split us up. I told you!" I thought, *Man, you're right.* At the same time I believed Rodney Peete had something we needed, and that was how I addressed the situation to Randall.

"It's not about our relationship," I said. "It's not about trust. It's about the performance. It's about what this team needs now. We need a spark. We need a guy that can give us different leadership."

I tried to sell that to Randall. Although he didn't take to it very well he was professional about the way he handled being a backup. He listened to what we said in meetings. He stayed into the game plan. He got killed in the media, of course, as people lined up to take their shots at him.

The 1995 season would be Randall's last in Philadelphia, but a couple of years later he signed with Minnesota and really tore it up in 1998. I was happy for him. Even now, whenever I see him at a golf tournament or another function, I feel bad about the way it ended for him in Philly. Probably one of the biggest letdowns of my career was not helping Randall enjoy success in this system.

After the '95 season I met Bruce Allen, a senior assistant with the Raiders, at the Scouting Combine. Bruce told me that Al Davis, the team's owner, wanted to talk with me about becoming the coordinator for the Raiders, who at the time were coached by Mike White and who already had Joe Bugel running their offense. I asked Ray to give the Raiders permission to talk with me—which he did—because if nothing else it would provide the chance for me to meet Al Davis for the first time.

"I have to do this," I told Ray. "This is THE guy, a legendary figure in NFL history. I have to meet him."

The Raiders had returned to Oakland from Los Angeles in 1995, but they flew me to LA, where I sat down with Mike and Joe, who told me he was going to remain the coordinator.

"Well, if you're the coordinator, then what am I here to be?" I asked.

"You're going to be the quarterbacks coach and you're going to call the passes while I call the runs," Joe said. "We'll work together and we'll put together an offense."

I had a lot of reservations about an arrangement like that because Joe was a smart coach who had his own ideas of what to do on offense. The last thing I wanted to do was go out to California and ruffle anyone's feathers.

The next morning Bruce Allen and I flew from LA to Oakland, where we would visit Al Davis's house. Most of the conversation was about offense. He wanted to know what plays I liked in the red zone, what I would call on fourth-and-goal from the three-yard line. He wanted me to draw up some patterns, to tell him what kinds of protections I would use against zone blitzes. He talked a lot about his offensive philosophy, which emphasized attacking opponents with a vertical passing game and differed greatly from the "West Coast" approach I was more comfortable with.

Still, I was totally in awe to meet Al and talk about football with him. It was unbelievable. Although I didn't feel good about taking the job because of the possible conflict I thought there might be with Joe Bugel, I appreciated the shot to interview for it.

I can't begin to describe how bad a stadium the Vet was. You had all sorts of creatures crawling around the place at all hours of the day and night. Most of the time you hoped they would never get too close for you to find out what they were, but even if you couldn't see them, you could hear them. You also could smell them, along with every other foul odor that just collected in the place through the years.

Each night the coaches would have a catered dinner delivered while we were working, which is pretty much standard procedure around the league. Thursday night in Philly would always be a little more special because that was when we got chicken wings and barbecued ribs from Outback Steakhouse. Thursday night also was when the offensive coaches would watch tape of the opponents' red-zone defense. We'd be staring at those red-zone plays and thinking about that Outback delivery showing up at any minute.

You knew exactly when it arrived because it was the only pleasant smell breaking through the normal stink. You could hear the bags being ripped open as the serving area was being set up, and all you could think about was having one of those wings. Finally we just would drop everything and attack the food. When we finished we left our plates, piled with wing and rib bones, on the table for the maintenance people to take care of when they came in early the next morning. Now if you showed up at 3:30 or 4 A.M., as I did, you were usually there before the maintenance crew. That meant as soon as you turned on the lights four or five huge rats would start scurrying across the table where they had been feasting on all of those bones.

We'd be sitting in a quarterback meeting, watching film, and all of a sudden an exterminator would just walk in carrying a big metal can with a hose attached to it. He wouldn't say anything; he'd just start spraying all over the room. Rodney Peete would turn to me and ask, "What's he doing? Should we be breathing that stuff? Is it safe?" I didn't know what to tell him, but if it did anything to keep the rats away I was all for it.

The offices had drop ceilings, which were made of thin asbestos tiles that sat on metal frames. If a tile cracked, someone would just pop it out and replace it. Whenever it was quiet, early in the morning or late at night, you could hear things running back and forth inside the ceiling. Every once in a while you would look up at one of those white tiles and see a big, brown stain. You'd say to yourself, *What is that, man? How did that get on my ceiling? I don't remember throwing coffee up there. Maybe it was dirty water leaking from some pipe.* Then the more you looked at it, the more you could see that it was a pee stain—that something on the other side of those tiles was peeing on your ceiling.

We had a veteran running backs coach named Dick Jamieson, who was in his late fifties at the time. One day he opened the door to his office at about 5:45 A.M. I was in my office studying tape, and all of a sudden I heard Dick let out this loud scream: "Ahhhhh!" I thought maybe he had had a heart attack or something so I ran over to see what was wrong. It turned out that as soon as Dick opened his door a monster-sized cat came running out. We looked up at his ceiling, and sure enough, there was a big hole in one of those pee-soaked panels where the cat had come crashing through.

All kinds of crazy things happened at the Vet. I remember another morning sitting in my office when the security guy came down and said, "You need to come upstairs right now! Right now! You've got some bandits going through your car!" When I got up there I found that someone had broken into my car and taken whatever change I had for the bridge toll. That place was amazing. But sick as this sounds, I loved it. I loved coaching in Philadelphia. It was such a cool city, old school, hard-core. I especially loved the fans because you not only had fathers and sons who went to the games, but grandfathers, too. I had never seen anything like it.

You knew right away you were going to be judged there. You were going to be accountable for your performance. A good performance, and you might get slapped on the back. You might have somebody slide you a cold one down at the bar. But on bad days? You were going to hear about it from everyone everywhere.

One time I was down in the south end zone of the Vet watching pregame warm-ups, and from the stands behind me I heard,

"Hey, Gruden! You are a bleeping idiot!" Our players were laughing and high-fiving each other. "Hey, Gruden! You are a bleeping idiot!" This guy's voice was loud and clear, and the players were loving it. They were laughing so hard they could barely stay on their feet to go through the drills. You try to ignore it but you can't. At some point you've got to turn around and see who it is. I finally turned around and it was some guy wearing one of those green construction hard hats with the Eagles logo on it.

Another time, when I was taking my wife out to dinner at a nice restaurant a waiter came up and said, "The gentleman over there would like to send you this drink."

"Thank you," I said.

He handed me a beer and then he gave me a napkin. On the napkin was a note, "Have two more of these, hit the road and don't come back."

Gee, thanks.

Then you had all the Philadelphia writers, like Bill Lyon and Bill Conlin, who were going to have something to say about you. So were the famous Howard Eskin and the other talk-show hosts and callers on 610 WIP Radio. You couldn't escape it. You were going to be scrutinized. And I loved it.

It was a skin-thickening process, though. Those three years probably quadrupled my mental toughness. That first year was rough. There were days when I felt like the dumbest person on the planet, when I was ready to drive my car into a tree, when I felt like I was losing my mind. As we had more success and as I became more confident in what I was doing and more comfortable in the job, I was able to handle it a lot better. I learned how to get over it. It was a hell of a trait I acquired that would be very helpful throughout the rest of my career.

For whatever reason, Ricky Watters never really seemed to warm up to me. We had another back at that time named Charlie Garner. I called him "IO," instant offense. We tried like hell to get Ricky and Charlie in the game together, but whenever Charlie was carrying the ball and Ricky wasn't, there would be friction because Ricky would be pissed.

Ricky came from San Francisco, the Super Bowl champions, to Philadelphia to become THE guy. And he was. He carried the ball and caught the ball for more combined yardage with the Eagles than he had anywhere else in his career. You're talking about one of the game's fierce competitors, a player who is convinced that "If you give me the ball, throw me the ball, I'll win the game for you. And if you don't give me the ball and throw me the ball enough, you're an idiot."

To a degree he was right. At the same time there were other players whom we needed to use. We were playing Buffalo in 1996, and there was a series where we used a personnel grouping called "Rocket," which allowed us to get Garner and Watters on the field at the same time. We took the fullback out, moved Ricky to fullback and put Garner in the game. It ended up being a pretty good series for Garner; we had about three or four consecutive plays of eight or nine or more yards. While Garner carried the ball Ricky was in motion or he was blocking, but he wasn't carrying the ball. It really pissed Ricky off. From the field he was making all these angry gestures up to the press box. Everybody knew whom he was yelling at.

We weren't the 49ers when Ricky came to us. We were the Philadelphia Eagles, with an offense coached by a couple of guys still finding their way. We didn't have a Bobb McKittrick. We didn't have a staff that had been together for seven years. We didn't have Rice and Taylor. We didn't have Brent Jones at tight end. We didn't have seven, eight, nine years of continuity in the same system. We were teaching it from scratch. Maybe Ricky was ready for more, more, more, but maybe we weren't.

There were times after games when I'd go in there shaking

guys' hands and Ricky made a point to not even be near me when I was offering congratulations or whatever. It was tough. Of course Ray wanted to make sure that Ricky was the focal point while at the same time getting other players into the mix. But there was just no way to do that without Ricky getting all bent out of shape. It was an everyday deal.

Still, what a horse Ricky was. As much as maybe he didn't like me and maybe we didn't get along, he was a bitch of a football player and did he deliver for us. Had it not been for the way Ricky performed I don't think any of us from that coaching staff would have had the opportunity to go on to do some of the things we were able to do.

Five weeks into my second season, in the second quarter of a Monday night game against Dallas, we lost Rodney for the season with a torn patellar tendon. Ty Detmer, who had come to us that year after spending four seasons as a backup in Green Bay, took over. Ty had never thrown a pass in the NFL, but we were still rolling on offense. In the second half Ty got drilled by Darren Woodson and he was staggered. He was out on his feet and the trainer was ready to have him sit out the rest of the game. I was against that because the only quarterback left was a rookie, Bobby Hoying, so I yelled at Gerald Carr on the headset, "He's all right! He's all right!"

The doctor came over to take a look at Ty on the sideline. To check Ty's mental capacity the trainer wanted Gerald to ask him some football questions. Gerald started to ask what the formation was on Brown Right A Right, which I knew, in his groggy state, Ty would have a hard time answering because it was one of our more complicated plays.

"No!" I told Gerald on the headset. "Ask him what the formation is on 22 Hank."

That was more generic and would give Ty a better chance to

get it right. Gerald asked it and Ty, while slurring his speech a little, knew the answer: "Red right."

"What's the formation on 23 Z In?" Gerald asked.

"Red left," Ty said, still slurring his words.

"See, he's fine," I said. "He's okay. Let him play."

Ty went back in and lasted about fifteen or twenty plays before he had to come out again. We gave it our best shot, but Hoying had to finish the game. He threw an interception on a Hail Mary pass on the last play and we lost 23–19.

Ty did come back to lead us to four straight wins. He played well enough for us to lead the NFC in offense and finish 10–6 for the second year in a row. We ended up going to the playoffs, facing the 49ers at 3Com Park in the wild-card round. That game was frustrating because we got the ball in the red zone three times in the first half on three great drives and got no points. It was pouring rain; the winds were gusting up to fifty miles an hour. Ty ended up leaving with a hamstring injury on our first possession of the second half, and Mark Rypien had to finish the game. We lost 14–0.

Getting knocked out of the playoffs in the first round was disappointing, but that was a hell of year we had in 1996. That might have been as good a coaching job as Ray and I had been associated with. We had to overcome a quarterback injury as well as numerous other injuries, yet we still won ten games in the NFL and really had a chance to beat the 49ers in San Francisco. Had we not turned the ball over and done some other crazy things in the red zone, maybe we would have won that day.

As I was driving to work the next day I was listening to WIP and some guy called in and said, "Jon Gruden . . . if his IQ was one point lower he'd be a plant. He's worthless. He's a moron."

The host agreed with him, of course.

•

After that second season I ran into Bruce Allen again. The Raiders were looking for a head coach, but Bruce said they wanted to talk with me again about being the offensive coordinator.

"No," I said. "I only want to interview for the head coaching job. I have a coordinator's job. We've been to the playoffs two years in a row. I already interviewed for a coordinator's position with the Raiders. Now I want to interview as a candidate to be head coach."

The next day Bruce called.

"What we talked about yesterday?" he said. "You've got it. You're going to interview for this head coaching job."

I flew out to California again, but this time straight to Oakland where I met with Bruce before heading over to Al's house for the interview. We sat out by Al's pool and he pulled his chair close to mine, to where we were sitting practically face-to-face. We talked about everything—the philosophy of the offense, the philosophy of the head coach, the history of the Raiders and the vision of the organization as he saw it as the owner.

Al's interview was not like any I had ever been through before. He changed gears constantly. His questions went from left field to right field, from shortstop to second base. His interviewing technique was magnificent. It was a stimulating, awesome line of questioning from a man who knew all there was to know about the NFL, including the salary cap, which other owners, club executives and coaches still have a hard time figuring out. He had seen it all in football.

"What are the most important positions on a football team, and how would you rank them in terms of their priority?" Al asked me.

I obviously put quarterback as number one. Blue-chip pass rusher was number two because that's a guy who can change a game, the offensive strategy. And because ninety percent of the quarterbacks in this league are right-handed, you want that rusher coming from the right side of your defense, which is the quarterback's blind side.

Left tackle and shutdown corner tied for number three. You need the tackle to line up against that great pass rusher, and when you put that shutdown corner on a lesser receiver, you can double the opponent's best receiver and just be more creative in your defensive scheme. Fourth was a stud receiver—a guy who can catch the low ball, catch the high ball, create a big target to throw at, come out of trash, make a short pass a big gain.

There's not one position where you can afford to have a weak link, but some are more important than others. Al also asked me about the kinds of traits I look for in players: "Do you like little linemen, athletic guys? Do you like the big, massive, zone-blocking brutes? What kind of vision do you have for the halfback position? What kinds of things do you want to see in your quarterback? Is it the vertical game? Is it the decision making? Accuracy? Touch?"

Then he got into special teams. "If you've got all these star players," Al asked, "who's covering the kicks?"

I wasn't told whether I had the job or not when they put me on the plane back home. I got another call from Bruce to inform me that Al wanted to interview me again, this time in New Orleans, where he was for Super Bowl XXXI between Green Bay and New England. I met with Al in his hotel suite and I thought I did as well as before, even though he still wouldn't say whether I was hired. As I left New Orleans I thought, *I'm going to get this job. It was my second interview. He must think I'm the right guy to interview me twice.*

I returned to our family vacation in Tampa and while I was on the beach throwing a Frisbee with my oldest son, Deuce, my wife, Cindy, yelled to me that I had a phone call. It was Al Davis.

"Sorry, Jon, but we're going to hire Joe Bugel," he said.

"Well, I appreciate the interest," I said. "Thanks a lot for calling."

I was crushed. I really thought I had a viable shot. But I did appreciate the fact that he gave me the chance to get in front of him for a head-coaching job. It just wasn't my time.

In our first two years in Philly we won twenty-one games, including the playoffs. Ray Rhodes won Coach of the Year. We had two quarterbacks coming back who had won in Rodney Peete and Ty Detmer, and young quarterback we liked in Bobby Hoying. We had Ricky Watters, Charlie Garner and Irving Fryar at receiver. We had good players.

Then, all of a sudden, free agency came along and we lost Bill Romanowski, an outstanding linebacker, to Denver after the '95 season. William Fuller, a powerful defensive end and our leader, ended up going to San Diego after the '96 season. Ricky Watters, who had had three magnificent seasons, was going to become an unrestricted free agent after the 1997 season, and there was no indication he would be re-signed. Charlie Garner was due to become unrestricted a year later, and there was no indication he would be re-signed, either.

We went 6–9–1 in '97. As poor as that record was, we actually played pretty well. Bobby Hoying got his first chance to become a starter through the final six weeks, and I'm proud to say he made the most of it. He even won NFC Offensive Player of the Week honors after throwing for three hundred yards and four touchdowns against Cincinnati. We just had some bad breaks that proved to be the difference in keeping us out of the playoffs for the first time in three seasons. I can't think of many bigger heartbreaks than the one we had in week three on *Monday Night Football* in Dallas. We're down 21–20 and Freddie Solomon catches a forty-six-yard pass to set up a chip-shot field goal with four seconds left. What happens? We fumble the snap. Game over. Even after going 6–6–1, we still were only a game out of first in the NFC East. A win over the Giants would have put both of us at the top of the division. We ended up losing

31–21, yet we had a shot a wild-card berth if we beat our final two opponents, Atlanta and Washington, and got some help from a couple of other teams. But back-to-back three-point losses brought my third year in Philadelphia to a bitter conclusion.

I felt it was time to move on. As long as the team was undergoing changes, I thought I might as well do the same.

# NINE

# If the Head Coaching Jacket Fits, Wear It

## Silver, Black, and Fearless

Hanging loose at the Pro Bowl with Rich and Shelley Gannon and my wife, Cindy. (Courtesy of the author)

**F**OR THE THIRD OFFSEASON in three years I was sitting down with Bruce Allen. For the third offseason in three years he was saying the Raiders wanted to interview me because their head coaching job was open again.

"I'll go for it," I said.

I took another trip to Oakland to meet with Al Davis. Bruce knew I respected Al and the Raiders and their place in NFL history. Al Davis might be the one guy I've met who loves football more than I do—or at least as much as I do. Football is all he does. The Raiders are all he cares about. A lot of people like golfing, they like going to the beach, they like sitting in the sun, they like going to concerts. Al just involves himself with football and he doesn't want to do anything but win. BIG!

There really was no way I could make sure I was any better prepared than I had been for our other interviews. You can't prepare for an interview with Al Davis. There are no self-help books or seminars that can show you how to make a favorable impression on him because he has his own way of doing things and it just isn't something that can be communicated in a textbook explanation. One way or another, Al's going to find out if you know football. He's also the only one who is going to determine whether you do or you don't.

The reason I think he needed to interview me as many times as he did was that I was an outsider. I wasn't a lifelong Raider like previous head coaches who had also played for Oakland—

Tom Flores and Art Shell—and when they went outside the family, so to speak, things just hadn't worked out as well. Also, at thirty-four, I was very young. Tossing the keys to the Oakland Raiders to someone like me in those times, when their team had fallen a little bit, was a real risk.

Whether it worked out or not, I saw it as another step in my Harvard-quality football education. To that point I had been around some of the greatest coaches and front-office people in the game. How about Al Davis? Let's go see what this world is like. Let's be judged by him. He'll let me know if I'm good enough or not.

Although I wasn't officially hired yet, Al asked me if I could stay in town for a couple of days and stop by the Raiders' offices, which were only a few miles from my hotel, to watch some of their videotape from the previous season. Afterward he and Bruce would ask my opinions of the team's personnel. We were going over some really inside things—how many picks they had in the coming draft, who the free agents were, what the salary cap looked like—that made me feel that I had the job even if I didn't officially have it.

I would go back to my hotel room at night with a Raiders' jacket and other team gear Bruce gave me, then return to the offices the next morning to watch more video and answer more questions. I didn't know if I was still interviewing or if I had the job or anything. I was just basically going with the flow. I was very much excited about being there and was willing to do almost anything to get that job. Some nights I would put on that Raider jacket and look at myself in the mirror in my room and think, *Man, this is really something!*

After a couple of days, I met with my agent, Bob LaMonte, who then headed over to the Raider offices. Soon thereafter, I got a call from Bruce Allen. A three-year contract was ready for my signature.

•

Getting a head coaching job didn't really give me a lot of juice to jump up and down and say, "Oh, this is great!" It's not like it guarantees you anything except one game, maybe one offseason. You've got to get results.

As I understood it Al basically wanted a different approach at that point. He wanted to get some new ideas in the mix. I think he wanted to keep his core philosophy in place, but there was a sense that he was looking for a fresh start for the Raiders—that they needed to do something different from what they had been doing.

I also think Al understood that I didn't have a lot of concerns or fears based on what had happened in Philadelphia. Here I was, a young guy who had done a decent job of coordinating offenses and after only his third year into it he was willing to take a chance to find a greater challenge and more responsibility. I went in there with the state of mind that I was not at all worried about having Al Davis run me out of town because at least I had a chance to be judged. I was not worried just because he would be at practice or wanted to sit in on staff meetings. I wasn't a cocky guy, but you've got to be yourself. You've got to be all you can be while you're there.

I had studied hard. I had been around great, quality people. This was my chance. Now that I had it, I was going to do the things that I knew how to do. I couldn't come in and have minicamp the way the previous two head coaches, Joe Bugel and Mike White, had minicamp because I didn't know how to do it their way. I didn't know how to coach a certain play or a certain protection other than the way I had learned. And by God, we were going to do it hard.

For three years in Philadelphia I had helped organize our off-season program and training camp schedule in terms of what we practiced, when we practiced it, the installation of the offense. I helped set up our year-round calendar. When I was Mike Holmgren's assistant in Green Bay I spent a lot of time making sure that all the offseason dates worked within league policies. I didn't have the authority to make the final decisions in either place, but I had learned about what went into that kind of organization. When I was with San Francisco, I had taken copious notes about hitting the seven-man sled the first three or four days of pads. I had learned about making sure that when the horn blows in practice, everyone knows where to go and moves briskly to the next drill. I had discovered the value of videotaping the coaches' installation of the offense, so that those classroom lectures would be accessible in the future when new players and coaches came aboard.

The things that I witnessed were things I was going to do in Oakland. We were going to do all of it, including the way we traveled in San Francisco. If a player wants his own room, a player can get his own room. I was with the players a lot in San Francisco and they loved the way the 49ers practiced, which was often without pads because it helped keep them fresh and extend their careers. I learned that happy players usually are more productive players.

Until I got to the Raiders, they never did their game plans on computers, which we had started doing in San Francisco. The Raiders didn't have an Avid video system—now standard equipment for every team in the league—that breaks down game tapes into play catalogs that are easy to sort, giving you an instant video library. There were a lot of things that hadn't been done in Oakland before that we were going to do. We had a program that I had seen work with the 49ers. I saw Mike Holmgren turn the Packers around with that program. When we put that program in at Philadelphia, Ray Rhodes won Coach of the Year.

There were a lot of things I was experiencing for the first time—running meetings of the entire staff, disciplining players, thinking about what to say to the whole team, making sure I was visible enough to the defensive players and the special teams, which is an area I could still improve on to this day because of my commitment to being an offensive guy. The way I've always tried to stay involved with our defenses in Tampa and Oakland is to try to rip them every day in practice with six completions in a row, nine completions in a row and then tell them, "We're going to get eleven tomorrow!" They love spitting right back in my face, saying, "No completions today! No yards for you today!"

Another new area of responsibility was dealing with the media, something you don't have to do on a regular basis as an assistant. The Raiders have a certain way with the media. Basically they don't want you saying very much. When I got the job, some of the team's administrators put me through a forty-five-minute mock press conference the day before the actual press conference introducing me as the new head coach. I stood at the podium and they asked me questions that they believed the media would ask me. After I gave an answer they would tell me a different way I could say something or what I should include in a particular comment. They wanted certain themes to be projected to the fans and to the world. They also pointed out that I was talking to our players as well. It was a good experience and helped me to get better in that area. For the most part I tried to be myself but I didn't elaborate on some issues as much as I might have otherwise.

But I had been around football my whole life. I had been around enough team meetings led by great coaches. It wasn't as if I had no idea what to do. Even if you're an assistant coach, after you listen to what the head coach has to say in a team meeting, you think, *Those were some great points he made in there.* Or you might walk out of the meeting and say, *I wish he would have jumped that guy's ass.* Or *I wish he would have given that guy some more credit.* Or *I wish he would have been more specific.* You have an idea of what needs to be said. You're not oblivious.

I also was kind of eager to learn about doing things the Raider way, about the family tradition that is encouraged throughout the franchise. I was asked if I would mind legendary former players—such as Jim Plunkett, George Blanda, Ted Hendricks and Tom Flores, who also was a Super Bowl–winning coach for the Raiders and part of their radio broadcast team—being around the building. I guess some coaches didn't feel so good about having those guys around, but I loved it. In fact, every year in the offseason I'd have a "legends dinner," a little get-together at a steakhouse where we'd bring in guys like Clarence Davis, Jack Tatum and George Atkinson. I wanted to learn about the history and tradition of the Raiders. That was what we wanted to return to. I was fired up about that. I bought into that wholeheartedly.

Of course, none of the preparation or studying I did could have ever prepared me for what happened to Leon Bender, a big defensive tackle we drafted from Washington State with the second-round pick we received that year after veteran defensive tackle Chester McGlockton left us to sign with Kansas City. Two weeks after we signed Leon to a contract, he had an epileptic seizure and died tragically at the age of twenty-two. Although I was a young coach and a head coach, that just showed me how vulnerable we all are. This was a young guy, full of life. He was a husband, a father. We were looking at him and our two first-round picks, cornerback Charles Woodson and offensive tackle Mo Collins, as building blocks for the future. And in an instant all those hopes and dreams disappear, and there's nothing left but sadness and tears.

I wasn't kidding myself about the job in front of us. Not only were the Raiders coming off a 4–12 season, they ranked near the bottom of the league against the pass, against the run and in total defense. We had questionable morale on the team. When I got there I found only six guys working out.

Without trying to sound arrogant or cocky, we had a lot of confidence that we could lead this team and that we could help this team improve. I knew the offseason schedule we were going to put together was demanding. We were going to be a more disciplined team. And the owner was committed to getting us players. That was one thing that fired me up about the job. I knew Al Davis was going to get players.

I planned to have a minicamp about a week after I was hired. As soon as Bruce Allen saw that on the calendar he said, "You can't have a minicamp this soon. We only have twenty-four players under contract." At the time, the Raiders still had to adjust their salary cap, but I was going to have that minicamp as scheduled. Our personnel department ended up having to sign about fifty guys from a three-day tryout camp just to give us enough bodies for the workouts. Some of them had played in the NFL, but some of them looked like they had never put on a helmet.

Jeff George, our quarterback, was throwing quick outs, hitches and slants. Tim Brown would catch one. James Jett would catch one. The next guy up was from the tryout camp and Jeff almost killed him, almost knocked his head off with the ball.

I was going to get to know the players. I wasn't going to say a lot, but the message I delivered would be "We're going to bust our asses and you're going to be accountable for how you play. I don't really care if I'm here ten days or ten years. We're here to turn this sonofabitch around and we're going to do it. If you're with me you're with me. If you're not you're not."

I liked Jeff George. During our first minicamp he moved to his right and threw a pass from his hip thirty-eight yards on a rope that Olanda Truitt caught right at his Adam's apple. It was unbelievable. I looked up at the video guy in the sideline tower and asked, "Did you get that on film?"

"Yes," the guy said.

"Good. Because that's the greatest throw I've ever seen."

The Raiders were Jeff's third team at that point. The Colts had made him the top overall pick of 1990, then traded him to Atlanta in 1994 for a couple of first-round picks. He had a lot of talent as a passer. He came to Oakland as a free agent in 1997 and was the top-rated passer in the AFC that year and first in the league with 3,917 yards passing.

The offense Bill Callahan and I put in was the one I had been studying since I was in San Francisco, but with a Raider spin on it. For instance we'd use "Casper" for a comeback route, after Dave Casper, the Hall-of-Fame tight end. The concept was basically the same, although Jeff looked at quarterbacking differently from the other guys I had seen run this offense well. He would look way downfield and say, "I can make that throw," where a lot of other quarterbacks would say, "No way. It takes too long. I'm going to get hit by three guys before I ever get the pass off. I'm going to check it down to a shorter route right here."

In seven-on-seven drills, where there wasn't any pass rush, I don't know if Jeff ever checked the ball down, but you'd see him throw a seventy-one yard pass that hit a guy right on the screws. Everybody would be oohing and ahhing—the crowd, the writers. You'd hear people saying, "This guy's really a good fit for your offense." And all I could think was *We're in for a rude awakening*. As a coach, you knew the reality of the situation as you watched the tape: *Every one of these is a sack. We're never going to get any of these off. We've got to throw a wide flare. We've got to throw the ball in the flat right here.*

We got ripped in our first game against the Chiefs, who sacked Jeff ten times. Between injury and inexperience, we struggled on the offensive line, which didn't blend well with a pure pocket passer who was always standing in there looking for the big fish. That was why the Raiders had brought Jeff there—for that vertical game. And my understanding of offensive football was a big reason that the Raiders brought me in. After we scored eight points in my head coaching debut, I knew at that meeting the next morning all our players and coaches were going to be looking at me saying to themselves, "Oh, Mr. Offensive Guru. Nice game, loser. What have you got to say to today?"

I remembered what Mike Holmgren went through when he began his head coaching career at Green Bay. We lost by a field goal in our opener at home against Minnesota. We went down to Tampa and got destroyed 31–3. And there we were in our third game, trailing Cincinnati at Lambeau. Our starting quarterback, Don Majkowski, was on the ground with a twisted ankle. In comes Brett Favre—who has just joined the Packers and doesn't know very much about the plays, formations or anything else about the offense—and he ends up throwing a bomb to Kltrick Taylor to win the game. Brett's performance had a lot to do with us going 9–7 that year, but the biggest thing I noticed was that Mike never changed. I remember watching him install game plans with the same confidence, whether we won or got our asses kicked. His approach and his personality remained the same. I drew a lot from that.

In the second week Jeff came back to throw for three hundred yards to beat the Giants, who were the defending NFC Eastern champs. Denver, the defending world champs, beat us in week three, but we came back with another close win in Dallas. We were 2–2 after playing four damn tough games. Jeff was throwing the hell out of the ball. I felt we had a chance to be pretty good.

Then in our fifth game, at Arizona, Jeff suffered a badly torn groin muscle that would put him out for most of our final eleven games. We had to go to Donald Hollas, who had barely thrown an NFL pass to that point in his career. He actually did a decent job of keeping us competitive. He even got hot and won a couple of games in a row before a brief return by Jeff, who ended up reinjuring his groin muscle. With a lot of help from our defense we managed to salvage an 8–8 season.

The season seemed so much longer, with so many more peaks and valleys emotionally, than any other season I had ever gone through. As a head coach you're accountable for the play of the entire football team. It took a physical and mental toll, but I gained confidence because we did show improvement as a team.

I thought the morale on the team was on the rise. I thought we made great strides in coming together as a team and learning a new offense and a new defense. I thought our discipline, in terms of our practice tempo, was much better as the year went on. Guys were finishing plays, moving more explosively. It became more gamelike as far as the speed of the practice.

So despite the huge demands it placed on me, I'd have to say that first season was the most satisfying, because ultimately the responsibility fell on my shoulders.

# TEN

# Who's Chucky?

Some people think I look like a certain doll
that doesn't play nice.
(Tom Wagner/Tampa Bay Buccaneers)

Harvey Williams had 128 rushing attempts for us in 1998. I don't remember a whole lot about most of them, except for maybe two that were for touchdowns. The one running play I do remember the best wasn't for a score. It certainly wasn't for a big gain. In fact, it wasn't even a carry.

This was an attempt at an attempt, and it came during a 27–20 win against Seattle in what was then called Oakland–Alameda County Coliseum. Going into the game we knew that we were going to see a lot of weak-side blitzes, so we came up with an audible that would let Donald Hollas call a running play away from the overloaded side where the blitz would come from. When he said, "96 Seattle" or "97 Seattle" the back would know that he was going to get a handoff and run in the direction opposite the blitz.

As Donald stood at the line and called signals, he could see that the blitz was coming from the weak side. He called 96 Seattle. For whatever reason, Harvey ran 97 Seattle. When Donald turned to hand the ball off, no one was there. We had a busted play that made all of us—players and coaches—look stupid. It made us look like we didn't have a clue, and the crowd of fifty-one thousand let us know about it by booing.

I got pissed. I got mad. I just lost it.

"What the hell are you doin'?" I yelled as Harvey came to the sidelines. "Geez! We've been working on it all week. You know it's a blitz on that side. Why are you running over there?"

A few days later Harvey told a reporter about that encounter.

He said that when he saw me yelling at him he thought I looked like Chucky, the evil doll from the movie, *Child's Play*. In the next day's newspaper there were pictures of Chucky and me side by side. I had no idea the comparison would attach itself to me with the same relentlessness that the little psycho doll has for causing mayhem.

Until then I had never even heard of the movie. At first I didn't really give the comparison much thought because I've had people imitate some of my strange behavior ever since I started coaching. I've seen players in the locker room and in the back of an airplane kind of acting like me, doing my voice and hand gestures. A lot of coaches get that.

One of the greatest parts about the Coliseum is the "Black Hole," the south end-zone seats where the most rabid Raider fans—and there really aren't any other kind—can be found with their faces painted silver and black and the rest of their bodies covered in all of these wild, spiked costumes. I'd go on the field for pregame warm-ups and I'd hear them start chanting, "Gru-den! Gru-den! Gru-den!" I appreciated the support, especially after seeing how they got after the opposing teams. Besides, it was a whole lot better than what I had heard during some of those pregame warm-ups in Philly. So whenever I heard the "Gru-den!" chant, I would always turn around, run to the Black Hole and give them high-fives. When I did that before a game, not long after Harvey's comment and the Chucky picture next to mine in the newspaper, I noticed people in the Black Hole holding up Chucky dolls. After that I began to see more and more of them.

Like it or not, this was a nickname that wasn't going to disappear any time soon.

I've been accused of playing to the cameras, of knowing exactly when one of them will be zooming in, which is supposed to be my cue to start making all those crazy Chucky faces. Give me a break. When I'm on the sidelines during a game, I'm thinking about a million different things. I'm having conversations with the offensive coordinator in the press box and other coaches. I'm talking to the quarterback. I've got plays to call, options to consider, adjustments to make. The last thing on my mind is what kind of facial expression I'm going to make for the cameras.

If I'm closing my eyes or twisting my face, it's because I'm thinking, I'm concentrating—or I'm just pissed. I guess I've always been kind of a natural squinter anyhow. Sometimes it's out of sheer comfort to loosen the tension or whatever. It's also, in part, because I'm an animated kind of guy. A lot of guys in this business are animated. What's wrong with being animated?

I try to keep my cool, but it's hard for me. I'm an irritable person to start with. Then when I get to that stadium on that early bus and I get in my little room with my sideline sheet, I start feeling the excitement of the game. My heart's pumping at a pretty good pace. I feel a sense of anticipation as I start to think of all the situations that are going to come up. And when I get on that sideline and put on my headset, my mind just temporarily becomes somebody else's.

"Here we go! It's second-and-nine. They always blitz long yardage on second down. What? They didn't blitz? Goddang it! Why did I call that play?

"What are we doin'? What's the coverage? Ah, shit! We can't run! We can't throw! We can't tackle!"

Except for the language, it isn't a whole lot different from when I'm fishing with my oldest son, Deuce, and he catches a nice big blue gill, or when he caught his first bass. I get excited, man. When we get that bass on a hook and get him out of the water and then we lose him? I'm saying, "Ohhh! God! Geez! Man, we had him."

I'll also admit that some of the language I use on the sidelines, especially when I'm yelling at the officials, is bad. When the cameras do catch me saying a foul word, that's seen by a lot of people. I've received some letters of complaint, and as a result I've done a better job recently of trying to keep my language under control.

But I've never scripted anything as far as my facial expressions or what I've said to my team. Everything I do and say is from the heart. I'm a passionate guy. I love football. The title of this book is, for me, the reality of it. There is nothing I hate more than a lack of effort, such as when it comes to studying the game plan, because you're letting the rest of the team down. This is a team game. If you're not going to be all over that game plan and you're not going to execute your assignments on Wednesday, on Thursday and on Friday, how in the hell are you going to do it in a live, physical combat like you have on Sunday afternoon? You aren't.

I try to portray the kind of mentality I expect from the players every single day. I've tried to do that my whole career. As a receivers coach and as an offensive coordinator, I was responsible for setting the tempo of the offense, for the quickness of our attack. In practice I'd be yelling, "Get in the huddle! Get out of the huddle! Hurry up! Finish plays! Run down the field! Simulate making a long run! Practice breaking tackles!" I wanted the defense to know, "At least this guy is demanding."

But I never meant for my behavior to turn into a case of seeing all these Chucky dolls dressed in Bucs' outfits or whatever. I've seen people show up at training camp with their kids dressed like Chucky. I've got people sending me Chucky videos so that I'll sign the containers; that's a little extreme.

I don't think the comparison is a negative thing, although when I finally saw the movie it was clear right away that he wasn't a really good guy. Put it this way, it's not something I'm going to watch with my kids, that's for sure.

From that first season in Oakland, Al Davis was very involved in everything we did. He would call me at home sometimes or he would come by the office two or three times a week late at night with four or five plays he wanted to go over with me on videotape.

Al wore distinctive cologne that I can smell to this day. I knew he was coming down the hall before he ever got to my office. Al called me by a nickname, too, but it wasn't Chucky. It was Butch, although I never knew why. He'd say, "Butch, did you see the right corner on this play?" I'd fast-forward the tape and watch the play with him to see what the cornerback was doing, or not doing, that bothered him. Or he'd ask, "Butch, did you watch the left wing on the punt team? We're going to get every punt blocked."

At first I looked at such comments maybe negatively, like he was questioning every single thing we were doing. Then I started looking at it as if I were Al and I owned the team and it was all I cared about. I started thinking I'd probably be the same way.

Jeff George had an option in his contract after the '98 season, and we didn't pick it up, thus allowing him to become a free agent. There were a couple of other free-agent quarterbacks available whom we were interested in—Rich Gannon, who had been with the Chiefs, and Trent Green, who had been with the Redskins. The 1999 draft also was going to be a big one for quarterbacks with Tim Couch, Donovan McNabb, Akili Smith, Daunte Culpepper and Cade McNown expected to be first-round picks—which they were.

Gannon was thirty-three years old and had kind of bounced around the league. But he had played well against the Raiders, and Al Davis and Bruce Allen wanted me to take a look at him. When I watched his game film, I saw a great athlete; he was always a threat to run the ball. I saw an accurate passer. The bottom line was that the guy was a winner. Back when I was in Green Bay, Rich beat us when he was quarterbacking Minnesota. For whatever reason, the Vikings traded him to Washington and then he ended up in Kansas City. But he played on a scoring machine in Minnesota. In '98, Elvis Grbac got hurt and Rich Gannon took the Kansas City Chiefs to the playoffs and played very well, even though they started Elvis in the playoffs. Rich's touchdown-to-interception ratio was good and he was almost impossible to sack. You ask any player or coach in Kansas City, the Chiefs would have followed Rich Gannon right into the Gulf of Mexico because he was an awesome leader and they believed in him. Paul Hackett, the Chiefs' offensive coordinator at the time and my former boss at Pitt, gave Rich a ringing endorsement.

When I first met the guy I knew he was exactly what our team needed. He had a confident, detailed vibe about him, and we hit it off right away. It all went back to my answer to Al's question about what the most important positions on a football team are: the quarterback, the speed rusher, the left tackle, the shutdown corner. We had Charles Woodson and Eric Allen to take care of the corner position. We addressed left tackle the best we could with Mo Collins, another of our first-round picks the previous year. We were still looking for that speed rusher.

But for me to be the head coach of the team, we needed a quarterback who was kind of an extension of me, who would agree that if a pass protection we had called was going to be a problem against a particular blitz look, we were going to change to what was going to be a good play for that situation. We needed a quarterback who was going to practice at a high tempo and who was going to understand that we were going to throw the ball on time and accurately and who understood that we were going to have total discipline in our pattern running, in our decision-making, in our footwork. Rich was that quarterback and we signed him.

Why on earth was he available for us—and everyone else—to sign? Who knows? All that really matters is your vision of the position. As long as you look at the film, meet the player, do all your research, talk to his ex-teammates, talk to his ex-coaches, look at his win-loss record, you're going to get the complete picture of the guy. It wasn't like I wouldn't teach him the offense, wouldn't coach him constantly or be with him every day. It wasn't like I didn't know exactly what we needed from the position. And Al liked Rich, too. He and other people in that organization respected Rich's ability as much as I did. I wasn't the Lone Ranger on this guy.

When it comes to judging any quarterback, it's all in the eyes of the beholder. Hell, look at Brett Favre. He was told by Atlanta he wasn't good enough. When I first met the guy in my first year in Green Bay, I had no idea why the Packers wanted him. My second year there, we drafted Mark Brunell on the fifth round, and in two years he appeared in two games before being traded to Jacksonville. My third year in Green Bay we signed Kurt Warner as an undrafted rookie free agent. Look at where he is now. Look at quarterbacks all over this league: Brad Johnson, Jeff Garcia, Trent Dilfer. Tom Brady was a sixth-round draft pick who became a Super Bowl MVP.

Who really knows about that position?

When you meet Rich Gannon there is a certain edge you get that this game is very important to him, so we instantly had that in common. And I wanted people to jump on board with our kind of over-the-edge attitude. Maybe we were over the top. Maybe Rich and I did overdo it. It was a great match for me because he was a challenge to coach. He wanted answers and he wanted them right now. If the route was not run properly in practice, he wanted it corrected—or he was going to be on my ass. He wanted it to be right. He also was a lot like me in the sense that he wasn't afraid of being struck by lightning.

There wasn't enough football you could bring to Rich. He was amazing. If you had 150 passes in the game plan, he had every formation memorized. He made it look like he had practiced every play thirty times, even when he hadn't. You could install six brand-new plays on the practice field and he'd execute them like you had run them for six years. He had unbelievable ability to take what you showed him on the acetate out to the grass and get it done right.

We ended up spending a lot of time together. When I wasn't watching the defense or other drills in practice, I was with Rich previewing the next period or I was going over the period we just had. He kept almost the same hours I did. The doors to the facility would be locked when he arrived around 5:55 A.M., so we eventually gave him his own key to allow him to come and go as he pleased.

The room where we held our quarterback meetings was near the players' lounge, which had a pool table, a pinball machine and an arcade basketball game. We'd be in a meeting and Rich would hear pool balls being racked and guys striking them with the cue stick and finally say, "This is distracting to me." Rich took action. One night, when no one was around, he went into the lounge, grabbed all the balls from the pool table and hid them—in my office. They were buried deep under a pile of files. It took a year before I even knew they were there. Guys would go into the lounge looking to play pool, wouldn't find any balls and they'd leave. No more distraction.

In his constant pursuit of perfection, Rich sometimes rubs people the wrong way. Rich and I had our share of run-ins. People thought we didn't get along. Reporters would say that there was a rift between us. They couldn't have been more wrong. There wasn't and never has been any problem between Rich Gannon and me. I love Rich Gannon more than any guy I know. All I want him to do is be great.

We're just two type-A personalities. Put us together and sometimes you're going to have sparks and sometimes you're going to have fire. But there isn't a better guy alive than Rich

Gannon. He's just misunderstood by some people. And maybe I am, too.

I have something I call the "grit chart," which is a way of looking at your schedule in terms of the grit that's required to win each week. You have sixteen games, and every Sunday the difference between winning and losing is usually three to seven points. Very rarely do you see blowouts. That means to be successful you have to be a team that is willing battle the whole way, a team that has the grit to hang in there and make maybe one or two more plays than the other guys. We became that kind of team with Rich Gannon as quarterback. That whole first year he was with us we were in every game until the very end, beginning with the first two—at Green Bay and at Minnesota. Rich played well against the Packers, and we nearly won before Brett Favre, the very definition of grit, made a couple of big throws at the end to beat us. A week later we beat the Vikings in Minnesota. They were 15–1 the year before.

I just kind of marveled at what Rich had done in those two games. I thought, *We've got a chance with this guy. This guy's really good.* What I saw was what everyone now knows about Rich Gannon: His quarterbacking skills are unbelievable. He sees everything. He almost never makes a bad play. He's hard to sack. He rarely throws interceptions. He's accurate. And he can run.

Rich had two defining games that season. The first came in the middle of the year when he led us back from a 20–3 deficit to beat Bill Parcells and the New York Jets 24–23. In the final two minutes, he took us on a ninety-yard drive that ended with his five-yard touchdown throw to James Jett to win the game with twenty-six seconds left. Not only did Rich have 352 passing yards, but he also was our leading rusher with 60 yards, including a 36-yard gain that helped set up our first score.

The second defining game for Rich—and the launching point for the serious contender we would become over the next two seasons—was our last regular-season game of 1999 in Kansas City. It was Rich's Arrowhead homecoming. Before that the Chiefs beat the Raiders in eighteen of twenty-one games, including the previous five. They had humiliated us and they enjoyed it tremendously. We were 7–8. We were missing seven or eight starters due to injury. This game meant nothing to the Raiders because we were out of the playoffs. It meant everything to the Chiefs because if they won, they would win the AFC West outright and get a home playoff game. If they lost, they would be out of the playoffs and Seattle would win the AFC West.

Barely two minutes into the game, Tamarick Vanover took a punt eighty-four yards for a touchdown, and before we knew what hit us, we were losing 17–0 halfway through the first quarter. Their crowd was going crazy because they were on their way to winning the division and kicking the Raiders' asses—again. Then all of a sudden we got hot. Kenny Shedd blocked a punt and returned it twenty yards for a touchdown to make it 17–7. Napoleon Kaufman went the distance on a shovel pass. Rich hit a couple of screens in the two-minute drill as we drove forty yards to tie the game 38–38 at the end of regulation.

The Chiefs started overtime by kicking off out of bounds. We got the ball at the forty. We called Green Left Slot Fox 3 Z Bingo Cross, which we thought would be a good call if the Chiefs zone blitzed. It was a play-action pass where we sent Tim Brown on a crossing route, James Jett on a post route, Rickey Dudley clearing out the backside and two backs underneath to control the linebackers. They zone-blitzed it, both backs picked it up, and when they did, it left a big hole in the middle of the defense. Gannon hit Tim, who was wide open, on a basic cross for a twenty-four-yard gain. That put us in chip-shot field-goal range. Joe Nedney, who was our second kicker that season after replacing Michael Husted, made the kick to give us the victory. There was a state of shock in Arrowhead Stadium. You couldn't hear anything—except the Raiders celebrating.

We were 8–8 for the second year in a row, but once you see a team that never quits, a team that has the drive to overcome adversity, you know you've got a chance. Since 1998, when we lost 44–21 at Buffalo, we never lost a regular-season game by more than ten points through the rest of our time in Oakland.

After a dozen seasons in the league, Rich made his first Pro Bowl. It would not be his last. He inspired everybody. Just when it looked like we had no chance, Rich would duck a rusher. He'd throw a sidearm ball. He'd dive for a first down. His improvisation was amazing. He gave us a chance to win every Sunday.

As encouraging as that was, however, we also confronted tragedy after that season. Eric Turner, who had been an outstanding free safety for us, had missed six games of the '99 season because he was injured. Then, all of a sudden, he didn't take part in any of our offseason workouts. When I asked to visit with him, he refused and wouldn't say why. The next thing I know, he has intestinal cancer—something he didn't want anybody to know about—and I'm at his funeral in Southern California. That just stunned us, as Leon Bender's death had two years earlier. Two wonderful young people and outstanding football players taken away just like that.

Along with the acquisition of Rich Gannon, another highlight of those Raider years was signing Jerry Rice in June 2001. You're talking about the greatest wide receiver of all time, the owner of every major NFL career receiving record and ten Super Bowl records.

The day we signed him, Bruce Allen and I had a little golf outing with Jerry on the Ruby Hill course in Pleasanton, California. We played nine holes, then sat in a room by the pro shop and gave Jerry a package. He opened it up and there was a black jersey with a silver number eighty on it and RICE on the back.

Jerry was approaching thirty-nine at the time, and I never felt a greater sense of responsibility in my career than in trying to find a way to somehow coach him at a level where he was comfortable. We had moved him from flanker, where he had played during all those glorious seasons in San Francisco, to split end because Tim Brown was our flanker at that time. It was a transition for Jerry, a new learning experience, and I was nervous about that because I had such enormous respect for him.

A lot of our terminology in Oakland was carried over from what I had learned during my 49er and Packer days. For instance, if you call, "Red Right," the flanker lines up to the side of the call and the split end lines up on the opposite side. So in practice, we'd call, "Red Right" in the huddle, and Tim Brown would go to the right and so would Jerry Rice, because he had always gone to the right for sixteen years in San Francisco. We'd say, "Huddle up!" again. We'd call, "Red Right" again. And Jerry Rice would go to the right side. Again. He was just programmed to be a flanker, so we had to, in a certain sense, deprogram him. It took a couple of weeks for Jerry to learn how to do things the opposite of how he had done them for sixteen years. Until he became acclimated to his new position, he had to look at the formations as they were drawn up, hear them in the huddle and digest them.

But I had never seen anything like the work ethic of this thirty-nine-year-old Hall-of-Famer-in-waiting. He would get our practice scripts and through every second of the prepractice stretch, he would have a coach quiz him on the pass routes we were going to run that day. Between every period he would be off to the side, on one knee, concentrating and studying the next grouping of plays we were going to run. He hated making mistakes. He had so much pride in getting every detail right, it was amazing.

Look at what he's still doing as a player as he approaches forty-one. His success over such a long period of time is no fluke. It's all because of an unbelievable everyday work ethic. He's an amazing guy.

It was such a thrill, a rush to put together a seven-on-seven practice script knowing you had Tim Brown and Jerry Rice lining up against Charles Woodson and Eric Allen. When you put Jerry on the same team with Rich Gannon and Steve Wisniewski, you're going to have a chance to win every single game. I can't say enough about what a great experience it was to coach Jerry Rice.

After winning our division with a 12–4 record, we played the Baltimore Ravens in the 2000 AFC Championship Game in the Coliseum. We knew it was going to be a tightfisted game and we were still very much in it until it was over. The Ravens had a great defense. It was big, it was physical and it was talented. I remember looking at them in pregame warm-ups and thinking, *Look at the size of these linebackers. My God, they're huge!* They had Ray Lewis in the middle, and Peter Boulware and Jamie Sharper outside. They had two shutdown corners in Chris McAlister and Duane Starks. They had Rod Woodson at safety. They had those two big guys—Tony Siragusa and Sam Adams— in the middle. If you don't double them, you don't run. If you double them, no one gets to Ray Lewis. Even if you do get to Lewis, he just tramples people and makes the play.

But we had some pretty good players on our side, including the AFC's starting quarterback in the Pro Bowl—Rich Gannon. Unfortunately we wouldn't have him healthy, or even on the field, for the whole game.

Everyone remembers that Siragusa fell on Rich early in the second quarter. Everyone remembers that Rich left the game at that point with a separated left shoulder, but it wasn't Siragusa's 350 pounds that did Gannon in. Rich actually was injured on the third play of the game, the result of an error. The snap was supposed to be on two, but our center, Barrett Robbins, snapped it on one. Mike McCrary ran around the end unblocked because the left tackle was still in his stance. He landed on Rich, separating his shoulder.

Rich tried to play through it, but he was hurting. When Siragusa fell on him that was pretty much it. Bobby Hoying, who hadn't played all year, took over and threw an interception on his first pass. Rich tried coming back in the second half. He did everything he could to stay out there. It just wasn't going to happen, so he came out for good.

Without a healthy Gannon, we knew we were in trouble, although Bobby did do a good job of rallying us. He threw a touchdown pass to Andre Rison with about four minutes left, but it was nullified because Andre was called for offensive pass interference. We ended up losing 16–3.

That was a rough way to end a great season. It took a heavy toll. We had a chance to play the Conference Championship Game at home. You go to the stadium thinking Super Bowl. Our fans were fired up. The players were jacked. You're just not ready for the season to be over. But the next day there you are, handing out the offseason calendar. Guys are cleaning out their lockers, all going their separate ways. It's quiet. It's like death. It's terrible.

After that game the Raiders notified me that they were going to pick up a two-year option in the three-year contract I had signed in 1998. But I was realistic enough to know that I was still very accountable. I still had to get results. If I didn't, I would be gone. Reaching the AFC title game was nice, but all it really did was set the bar higher. We were expected to take the next step. I knew we had a good enough team to be very competitive again. With Rich Gannon at quarterback, I knew we'd be back.

We went 10–6 that next season. We won the AFC West again, but in losing our last three games we cost ourselves a first-round bye and home-field advantage in the playoffs. That meant we had to turn around five days later and play the Jets, who beat us in the regular-season finale on a last-minute field goal, again in the wild-card round. We played well and beat them, setting up a Saturday-night game in New England for a chance to go to the AFC Championship Game.

The snow was falling like crazy in Foxboro, Massachusetts. It's not supposed to be the kind of weather that a California team can handle, but we were the ones with the 13–10 lead with 2:24 left in the fourth quarter. We had a third-and-one from our own forty-four. We were a yard away from winning the game. We went to our signature short-yardage play, 14 Blast. It's supposed to work like this: Rich Gannon hands the ball as deep as he can to Zack Crockett, our short-yardage specialist. Zack runs right behind the lead fullback, Jon Ritchie, who blocks the onside linebacker. Steve Wisniewski pulls around the horn to block the backside linebacker. It's a great play. At least we thought it was. Much to our surprise, Bryan Cox came up to stuff it. No gain. We were still playing.

Our Pro Bowl punter, Shane Lechler, kicked a short punt. With no time-outs the Patriots got the ball at their forty-six. Tom Brady moved them to our forty-two. From that point forward, the whole country became very familiar with something called the "tuck rule." What we saw from our sideline was Charles Woodson blitz Tom Brady as he dropped back to pass. We saw Tom Brady fumble. We saw Greg Biekert recover it at our forty-eight. Our players are celebrating. We're going back to the AFC Championship Game!

But what we saw wasn't what the replay official upstairs saw. He challenged the fumble that the officials on the field had ruled. All of a sudden the game wasn't over. All of a sudden the fumble was an incomplete pass because after looking at the replay, the officials on the field said Tom Brady's arm was going forward to tuck the ball in. By rule, Charles Woodson knocking it out of his hand made it an incompletion, not a fumble.

We had one time-out left, but I wasn't going to use it. As a result, the Patriots had to send out their kicker, Adam Vinatieri, to try a forty-three-yard field goal with a moving clock. I didn't want to try and "ice" the kicker because I didn't want to give the Patriots' ground crew time for the same thing that had happened in that same stadium in 1982, when a work-release convict used a snowplow to clear a spot for John Smith to kick the winning field goal in New England's 3–0 victory over Miami. Vinatieri was kicking the ball literally out of five inches of snow, into the wind. He made it, sending the game into overtime. In overtime, Vinatieri kicked another field goal out of all that snow. Once again our season ended sooner than it was supposed to.

If my recalling this game is matter-of-fact, it's because it kills me to recall this sequence of plays. It should never have gotten to that point.

Now we went into the locker room. This was Eric Allen's last game as a pro football player. It was the last game Steve Wisniewski and William Thomas, a linebacker who had been with me in Philadelphia, would ever play in the NFL. What do you say? You've got guys who are so pissed, so mad, so upset. You've got guys feeling they've been cheated out of something.

Sure, if you coach, play or root for the Raiders, you can be all teary eyed about the "tuck rule," but I wasn't going to put that one on the officials. In my opinion, the outcome of the "Snow Bowl" will always come down to 14 Blast. You make that first down, the game's over. We got stuffed. There was some indecision up front about where Bryan Cox was going to be and maybe we didn't come off the ball as fast as we needed to. Whatever the reason, we didn't account for him and he came in to make the stop.

But the "tuck rule" didn't come into play until after we failed to convert a third-and-one, until after we got off a short punt. As I've always been taught, you get what you deserve.

•

After four seasons with the Raiders I entered the last year of my contract. My agent, Bob LaMonte, told me that negotiations for a contract extension were going nowhere. That meant I would be coaching in Oakland for another year, provided the Raiders still wanted me. I was prepared to honor my contract and do the best job I could for another season. I wasn't going to try to look any further into the future than that.

Little did I know that the biggest opportunity of my life was about to land on my doorstep.

# ELEVEN

# Changing Teams Doesn't Mean Changing Expectations

Celebrating with some of the greatest coaches around after beating
the Eagles in the NFC Championship Game. From left, Bill Muir,
Rod Marinelli, Monte Kiffin, me, and team physician Dr. Joe Diaco.
(Courtesy of the author)

I DON'T KNOW EXACTLY how I ended up in Tampa. Since the day I arrived here, I decided I wasn't going to look back. I was going to look forward and concentrate on whatever we had to do to make this team a Super Bowl champion.

But I can tell you that in mid-February 2002 I got a call from Al Davis at about one o'clock in the morning. The next thing I know, I've been traded. When I heard what the Buccaneers had agreed to give up for me—first- and second-round picks in 2002, first- and second-round picks in 2003 and $8 million—I just about fell on the floor. As I've said before, I wouldn't have given up a pair of size-9 1/2 turf shoes for me, let alone all those picks and all that money.

It isn't the sort of transaction that you typically associate with a coach, and I know everyone's got a lot of questions about exactly how it all came together. This isn't the place for me to address them. And frankly, I don't have all the answers myself. The bottom line was that I had been in a situation where I didn't know what my future would be beyond another season. I felt, if the right opportunity presented itself, it would be time for me to move on. Tampa was that opportunity.

"We're going to Tampa," I kept telling my wife, over and over, in the aftermath of Al's call.

Even as I said it, I'm not entirely certain I believed it was really happening. But it was. I thought about what the Buccaneers had meant to me and my family after my dad went to work for them in 1982. I thought about all the great times I had had in Tampa after my parents moved there when I started college. About going to training camp with my dad. Throwing passes to the backs he coached. Getting chased out of practice by Phil Krueger. Most of all, I thought about how good a team the Bucs were, especially on defense.

When the details were finally worked out, I had one final phone conversation with Al.

"Well, congratulations," he said.

"Thank you very much," I said. "It's been an honor working with you. I'll never be able to thank you enough."

"Good luck, Butch."

"Good luck to you, too."

The next call I made was to my dad.

"I'm the new head coach of the Tampa Bay Buccaneers," I said. He almost went through the ceiling.

It seemed almost unreal that I was going to be working at One Buc Place, where I had spent so much time while I was in college. I saw the old Coke machine that my dad had bought his Cokes from twenty years earlier. I saw the old showers that I used to shower in after sitting in the sauna—which was also still there—along with other coaches' sons acting like we were big-timers. Now I was back there as the head coach. Unbelievable.

I knew this wasn't going to be an easy transition. Tony Dungy, my predecessor, had done a hell of a job with the Buccaneers. They had been to the playoffs. They had built a great defense. With the Raiders having signed all the assistant coaches to contract extensions, I wasn't going to be able to have very many familiar faces working with me from that Oakland staff. One of those assistants, Bill Callahan, was promoted to replace me as head coach. I couldn't have been happier for him. Bill and I grew up together in this business. We share a lot of the same ideas about offensive football and the game in general. We're both just a couple of grinders who believe you can never study too much videotape.

The one guy I knew from the previous Bucs staff was Monte Kiffin, one of the great defensive coordinators in the league. Every summer I would take my wife and kids on vacation for three or four weeks to a beach bungalow on the Gulf Coast, and Monte had a beach bungalow about six units down from ours. Three or four times every summer we'd go out at night or we'd get up early and talk football. We became really close friends. One of the first things I did after taking the job was let Monte know I wanted to keep him and his defense. Monte has forgotten more about defense than I'll ever know.

Almost a month before I ended up in Tampa, Tony had become the head coach of the Indianapolis Colts. He had taken a lot of his offensive coaches to Indianapolis, so I had to fill most of the offensive staff. It wasn't easy because I got the job so late in the offseason. But we were fortunate to hire a good staff, getting some coaches from college and others with NFL experience.

One spot that had already been filled from the outside was offensive line coach. Bill Muir, who had long been one of the top line coaches in the league, was hired for that job, I guess, because of the expectation that Bill Parcells, who had some history with Muir, was going to be the Bucs' new head coach. I called Muir into the office and told him I wanted him to be our offensive coordinator. Bill said he didn't have to have the title, but I wanted him to because I knew he was a strong leader and a top tier offensive coach.

I also knew it would be a great challenge to earn his respect. He was a twenty-year NFL line coach. He had come from the Jets. He had worked with Bill Parcells. And considering that I came from an offensive background that might have been different from what he had been doing for the better part of his career up to that point, I'm sure he was looking at me with some questions. Most people who meet me for the first time—

hell, even most people who know me—usually look at me with a raised eyebrow anyhow. But I wanted to prove to Bill that I could do this job and I was eager to work with him because of his past experiences. It's funny how this business works. The Jets' offensive coordinator, Paul Hackett, whom I knew from my one season at Pitt, filled me in on what a superb coach Bill was, and it really helped me in dealing with him initially.

There were probably some defensive coaches on that Buccaneer staff who wanted to go with Tony to Indianapolis, so I had to sell myself to guys like Rod Marinelli, who coached the defensive line; Joe Barry, who coached the linebackers; Mike Tomlin, who coached the defensive backs. These are tremendous coaches and they were loyal. The defense they had put together was awesome. The one-gap system they use is, philosophically, a defense that I believe in wholeheartedly. You have four linemen, you get the hat in the crack and penetrate, disrupt, as opposed to a two-gap, "34" type of approach where you have three linemen and there is more reading and reacting. Both ways are effective, but I was from more of a one-gap lineage.

"I want this defense," I told each member of that defensive staff. "I don't want you to go. Please give me an opportunity to work with you."

Fortunately for me, they all decided to stay. I put a lot of trust in that defensive staff. I delegated a lot to them because I had great confidence in their abilities, and I let them know that. Through all the success I have witnessed on five NFL teams, the common thread is the strength of the assistant coaches. The head coach gets a lot of credit or blame when you win and lose, but the assistant coaches are critically important, and the group of coaches we had in Tampa was second to none.

After putting the coaching staff together, I met the players. I had to sell myself to them, too. A lot of them live in Tampa and some were around the office at that time. One of the first players I sat with was Derrick Brooks. He probably thought I was a weirdo because for the most part I just stared at him. I almost couldn't believe that I was going to have the chance to coach a team that had one of the greatest linebackers in the game. I couldn't wait to join forces with Derrick and John Lynch, the outstanding veteran safety; Warren Sapp, the best defensive tackle in the league; Simeon Rice, the game's best pass rusher; and Ronde Barber, a true shutdown corner if I ever saw one.

Lynch was one of the first Bucs players I contacted after I got the job. I called him at his offseason home in Del Mar, California. I couldn't wait to talk with him. I knew John was one of the leaders of that defense. I figured the only thing he knew about me was my reputation as an offensive guy and that he and the other guys on defense might assume that I wouldn't pay a whole lot of attention to them in practice. I wanted John and the rest of the defense to know what I was about. That was why, after we exchanged the usual pleasantries, I said, "Enough of the bullshit. I'm looking forward to that first minicamp when you walk down to that bubble on the weak side and I buzz a bleeping slant right by the back of your head. Enjoy your condo out there by San Diego, John. Relax. Go to the beach. We're going to be in here in working. We're programming our robots to defeat you."

I knew I had to earn their respect over a period of time, that I wasn't going to truly earn it in a fifteen-, twenty-, thirty-minute meeting. There was some hostility over the circumstances that created the head coaching vacancy there in the first place. The players loved Tony, and it was easy to understand why. He is a tremendous coach and a great person. That was a very sensitive locker room. Those guys had been through a lot, seeing all the reports in the media that Bill Parcells was going to be their coach. Then it was supposed to be Steve Mariucci. Now it's Jon Gruden? The search had gone on for a while and it was tough on them. I knew I had my hands full, but I also knew I had the support I needed from Monte Kiffin, Rod Marinelli and Bill Muir, to name a few.

At our first team meeting in the offseason I told the players, "I've got some big shoes to fill. You guys are on the brink of being a great football team. We've got to finish what we've started here, and I need your support. I need the veteran players . . . Derrick and Warren and John and Brad Johnson and Keyshawn Johnson . . . I need you guys to believe and trust in this program I'm going to implement here. I'm going to ask a lot of you guys.

"I'm going to be myself. I'm not like Coach Dungy. I'm going to be who I am and I'm going to try to earn your respect. But remember: Respect's a two-way street. While I'm trying to earn your respect, you've got to also work to earn mine.

"Tony's done a great job here and he's handed me the torch. I don't know how I got here, but I'm here. We've got a lot in common, men. I have some controversy following me, too. But I know you guys will like this program. I know you'll benefit from it. I've seen it work, guys, and together we can do this."

I also thought it was important to instill a sense of pride in the history of the Buccaneer franchise, which until recently wasn't all that illustrious for the most part. This was a team that went through some very humiliating times as an expansion franchise in the mid-1970s, going 0–14 and 2–12 in its first two seasons. Still, one of the great lessons from my Raider experience was the importance of promoting a family atmosphere around an organization, of making the former players—the guys who had blazed a hard trail—feel like they were still very much part of what the team was doing. I thought it was important that they knew they were very much appreciated even though they might not have always felt that that was the case. The fact my dad had coached and scouted for the Bucs in the 1980s gave me a special, personal bond—separate from what I now have as the coach of the team—that will stay with me my whole life.

So copying the idea of those "legends dinners" that we had in Oakland, I organized a private party for former Bucs' players. We had two of the quarterbacks—the great Doug Williams, along with Parnell Dickinson. We had Hall-of-Fame defensive end Lee Roy Selmon, as well as defensive linemen Brad Culpepper and John Cannon. We had tight end Jimmie Giles, defensive back Mark "Captain Crunch" Cotney, linebackers Richard "Batman" Wood and Scot Brantley and receivers Lawrence Dawsey and Kevin House.

It was our way of letting them know that we're proud of them. And I'll admit that, selfishly, I wanted to be reunited with some of these guys and get to meet the ones I didn't know, just like I wanted to meet those former Raider greats.

The first time I saw our defense on the grass in practice I knew it was good enough to take us to a Super Bowl. I take a lot of pride in coaching offense. Bill Muir does, too. We have a lot of formations. We have a lot of different schemes—runs, passes, no-huddle, trickery, whatever you want to do—and this defense was able to stop all of it. It is a very unforgiving defense. I knew that we could be just an absolutely unstoppable defensive team as long as we kept improving on offense and gave them hope that we could match their intensity, that we could feed off each other, that we could attack on offense as well as on defense. We wanted the defense to believe that if it would fight to get us the ball back, we were going to score.

I also had looked at a lot of the Buccaneers' defensive tape from 2001, paying particularly close attention to the turnovers. They had dropped about four or five interceptions, and three or four of them clearly would have been for touchdowns. They could have scored two or three more touchdowns on fumble recoveries. They ended up with two touchdowns on interception returns for the whole 2001 season, but the total should have been much higher.

"You should have had nine touchdowns," I said. "Not two or three, nine! When they throw it to you, catch it and run it back for a touchdown. When you've got a chance to scoop that fumble, run it in. We rush the passer, we create havoc, we get our hands on balls. We can score nine touchdowns. Score! Don't just get the turnover. Score! Nine touchdowns!"

The players were looking at me like I was crazy.

"Nine touchdowns?"

In our second game of the season, at Baltimore, Brooks returned an interception ninety-seven yards for a touchdown. A week later he scored again, on a thirty-nine-yard interception return against St. Louis. A week after that, Shelton Quarles had a twenty-five-yard interception return for a touchdown against Cincinnati. Three weeks, three defensive touchdowns. Now the players started talking about it. They began saying, "We're going to score on defense! We're going to score nine touchdowns!" Whenever the other team got the ball, our defense wasn't just thinking about keeping the offense out of the end zone. It was thinking about how it was going to produce points.

When Dwight Smith returned his second interception for a touchdown with two seconds left in Super Bowl XXXVII, that was the ninth time in the season our defense reached the end zone. One of the first guys to come up to me on the sidelines was Warren Sapp.

"You wanted nine?" he yelled. "You got nine!"

The thing you have to understand about Warren is that when it's all said and done, he just loves football. He loves to compete. He's relentless as hell. And he's a smart guy.

He's got a personality that never quits, a rolling ball of butcher knives every day. Every day is the same. Now, he's happier on some days than he is on others, but even when he's not a really happy guy, his motor is still going. He's in the left lane going ninety-nine miles an hour every single day. He sets the tempo. I love him.

What other player on that team—or in the NFL, for that matter—would come up with the idea of putting his head coach through a rookie-hazing ritual? You guessed it. Number ninety-nine. The only rookie hazing we do on the Bucs is make the top draft pick buy breakfast for the entire team the morning of the first home game of the regular season. We're not talking about some doughnuts and coffee. It's supposed to be a nice spread, prepared by a local restaurant, to the tune of a couple of thousand dollars. Sure enough, we were in a meeting before our home opener against New Orleans when Sapp looked right at me and said, "You're buying breakfast for the first two home games because you're our top draft choice this year *and* next year."

"You've got a point there, Warren," I said. "But I'm only doing it once because you only get drafted once, you know what I mean?"

Talk about a versatile athlete. We like to use Warren as a tight end in goal-line situations, not just because he's big and has great blocking ability but also because he can catch the ball. The guy has great hands. He was an All-American, all-world tight end in high school. Another reason I like having Warren in on goal line is that he's a detail guy. He gets off the ball on time. He's instinctive. He's physical. To have Warren and our regular tight ends, Ken Dilger and Rickey Dudley, on the field at the same time helps us.

One thing I want to make clear about Warren Sapp is that he is a legitimate football player. There is nothing dirty about Warren Sapp. I bring that up because in November he found himself in the middle of a controversy that seemed to put that in question. We were playing the Packers at home. Brian Kelly had intercepted a pass from Brett Favre and was on his way to the

end zone when Warren hit Chad Clifton, a tackle for the Packers, so hard on a block that Chad ended up in the hospital with
a serious hip injury.

After the game, as both teams were heading for their locker
rooms, there was a confrontation between Packers coach Mike
Sherman and Warren right in the middle of the field. We had
come from behind for a huge win that night over a team we
were fighting for home-field advantage in the playoffs. I didn't
even know what happened until after I got to our locker room,
but Mike and Warren ended up having words.

I didn't like that. I didn't like the way it portrayed Warren.
Warren is a great football player. He plays the game hard, every
down, and he plays it legally.

You never have to tell Warren or Brooks or Lynch or any of the
guys on our defense to run to the ball or finish the play. It's hot
as hell at our training camp in Orlando. I see people in the
stands literally melting in pools of sweat. And here are these
three-hundred-pound guys—with Sapp and fellow heavyweight
Anthony Mc Farland leading the way, along with Simeon
Rice—talking crap, talking trash, calling me "Blondie" and
"Chucky" and "Ducky." They're picking up our audibles,
saying, "Oh, no, not that one again." Then they run to the
exact place they need to be to stop a play. They're kicking our
asses on offense and they're loving it.

Of course, I do my share of agitating. I'll start off a practice
by saying, "We're going to perform surgery today on Derrick
Brooks. We're going to go after his ass." The first day of training camp we had a nine-on-seven drill. Usually every play in
nine-on-seven is a run. There aren't any receivers on the field, so
the quarterback is handing the ball off and you're running a
counter or a gap play or a zone play. The defense knows that a
run is coming. Everyone watching knows that a run is coming.
Well, on our first nine-on-seven play of camp, Lynch came

down on the weak side, looking for a handoff. Instead, Shaun King kept it on a naked bootleg. He ran for thirty yards. Lynch was just livid.

Lynch yelled at me, "That's a bunch of crap!"

"Yeah, Michael Vick's not going to run any nakeds against you and your lack of containment, is he?" I yelled back at him sarcastically. "No, he's not going to run eighty yards downfield. He's not going to run for three hundred yards on your ass. Do you think we should practice trying to stop some of those runs?"

That pissed off all our defensive guys. I've made it my mission to piss them off every day since because that's my way of challenging them, of keeping myself involved with what they're doing. Whenever we get a first down in practice, I'm yelling, "Beautiful! Keep after 'em! Keep ripping their ass!" I want our defenders to come out every day in practice looking to shut me up.

At first I think it was a little bit of a shock to them because they weren't used to having the offense or the head coach constantly coming after them in practice. They soon discovered that I was an equal-opportunity pain in the ass. They would hear me yelling at a wide receiver who busted an alignment or when the offense blew a scheme. I think they liked the fact that we all had accountability. We were challenging the offense to not only become a good offense, "but how about daring to become a great offense?"

I try to get to know my audience a little bit and try to stimulate the crowd I'm with. We have a lot of guys in Tampa who respond maybe a little differently from guys we had in Oakland. Not that those Raider players didn't respond, but nothing ever stays the same when you go from one team to another. I don't have a speech I give for opening games or for playoff games. I've just got to have an urge for what I think is appropriate for that particular situation at that particular time. It might be a case of using something that has just happened in society in general. Or sometimes I have too many cups of coffee on a given day and I'll come across a little strange.

What I say is never quite the same each time. I might talk about occasionally walking through a graveyard, reading the headstones and thinking about what sort of lives the deceased left behind. "One day that's going to be you, six feet under the ground, dead," I'll say to the players. "Are you going to do something before you die? Are you going to do something so that there'll be more than just dates on the tombstone to remember you by?"

I listen to a lot of rock and roll music. Sometimes, if I hear a good line, I'll write it down. Like in AC/DC's "Highway to Hell," there's a line that says, "No stop signs. No speed limits." Then I'll be on the practice field and if I'm not happy with the tempo, I might start yelling, "There's no stop signs, guys! There's no speed limits!" Wait a minute. Where have I heard that before? One of these days an AC/DC fan lurking on our team is going to say, "Hey, I know where that's from." It hasn't happened yet.

Now I realize there reaches a point where the players get a little sick of hearing from me all the time. I talk to the team during minicamp, during training camp, in the morning, after practice. To try to break up the monotony during the 2002 season, I gave some of our assistant coaches four games each to stand up once a week and address the football team. The first four games belonged to Rod Marinelli, the second went to Mike Tomlin and Joe Barry, the next four were Bill Muir's and the last four were Monte Kiffin's. Each coach would present a theme and give the keys to that week's game. As soon as the schedule came out, I told the coaches which games they were assigned, so they would do their research on the opponents. It was their chance to summarize the Saints, the Rams, and the rest of the teams on our schedule. What's it going to take to beat these guys?

I had never done anything like that before, but these are guys that I listen to, guys who give me juice all the time. It only made sense to let all the players hear from them, too. I just thought it would be a good way to generate some extra responsibility for our coaches while giving our players a different perspective and a chance to get to know our whole staff. I thought it would help us come together as a team and get away from having only the offensive linemen hear the offensive line coach and only the defensive linemen hear the defensive line coach and so on. Now the running backs could say, "Let's hear what the linebackers coach has to say."

Marinelli—whose shaved head, military backround and no-nonsense approach reminds me so much of Bobb McKittrick—started off the year by talking about a big rock.

"That rock is your opponent and you've got to keep pounding on it with a hammer," he said. "That rock is going to crack if you just keep pounding on it. You might not smash it the first four or five times. But you just think about one guy pounding that rock with a singular, tiny hammer. Then you think about two guys holding that hammer, pounding the same rock. Then you think about Warren Sapp showing up with his big howitzer hammer, smashing that rock.

"You think about pounding that damn rock all day, every day for four quarters. It's hot out. You're sweating. You're thinking, *That rock ain't gonna crack*. But you have to keep pounding that rock because it will crack."

At the end of every practice I always call on a different player to give us the break after we gather together in the middle of the field. Not long after Rod's speech, I started hearing each one say, "Pound the rock, on three! One, two, three, pound the rock!" The next thing I knew, players were talking about "pounding the rock" in the newspaper. I started seeing signs all over the stadium that said, "Pound the rock!" I saw T-shirts that said it. Everybody bought into that theme.

Four weeks into the season, Tim Sain, our equipment manager, actually brought a two-foot-long, ten-inch-high rock into
the locker room before our game in Cincinnati. It has become a
prominent and permanent symbol for our team ever since. Tim
cemented the rock to a nice blue base, and it comes with us
wherever we go. A lot of players make sure to touch it on the
way to the field while others just kind of look at it. Me? I rub it
carefully. I'm not going to reveal where Tim got the rock. That's
just going to have to be part of the mystique of the Buccaneers.

But I need help to lead. I can't be the Lone Ranger. I rely on
the coaches to give me some juice. The players do, too. And
they rely on each other for juice. Lomas Brown, an eighteen-
year veteran offensive tackle and the only guy we had who had
been in a Super Bowl (with the Giants), spoke to our team
down the stretch. We also heard speeches from Doug Williams,
the first great quarterback for the Buccaneers and someone who
went on to win a Super Bowl with Washington, and Ronnie
Lott, another major contributor to Super Bowl success with San
Francisco.

As we got ready for a late-season game against the Lions in
Detroit, I had Wayne Fontes, the all-time winningest coach in
Lions history and the ex–defensive coordinator for the Bucs
who lives in Tampa, come in to tell the players what they could
expect on their trip.

"Let me tell you something about Detroit," Wayne said in
his rapid-fire style. "They are tough to beat in Detroit. Those
Detroit Lions fans are passionate and they're going to stay with
them, so you'd better get off the bus ready to play." I can't put
the rest of what Wayne said in this book, but let's just say it had
a lot in common with some of Ray Rhodes's best speeches. By
the way, we beat the Lions 23–20. Thanks for the help, Wayne.

Probably the best two or three hours I spent at the 2002 Scouting Combine were at a restaurant with Norv Turner, talking

about Brad Johnson. Norv was beginning his first year as offensive coordinator of the Miami Dolphins, but when he was head coach of the Washington Redskins, Brad was one of his quarterbacks. In 1999 Norv saw Brad throw for 4,005 yards, the second-highest total in Redskin history.

"You're going to love this guy," Norv told me. "This is a real pro. He can make all the throws. He's got better movement than people think. He is tough as hell. You'll love him."

We had signed Rob Johnson as a free agent to give us some depth and competition at quarterback. We had a young guy in Shaun King, who had a little experience as a starter. While installing the offense in the offseason, we'd go outside to work with all three quarterbacks. I'd look at the grades at the end of the day, and next to Brad's name I'd see *complete, complete, complete, complete, complete . . . plus, plus, plus, plus, plus*. He rarely ever made a mistake. When he did, he never made the same one twice. He was just a consistent, improving football player who had an undying thirst for details. He gave me good feedback. He understood the game. He saw everything.

Brad is a quieter guy than Rich Gannon, but from a professional standpoint they're very similar. I respect Brad tremendously as a player. He makes helpful suggestions, such as pointing out a play that is similar to one he had run in Washington and talking about how he had executed it there. He accepts coaching. He absorbs a whole lot of football in a very short amount of time and executes well. He is a stud, man.

One thing we learned in talking with Brad was that he isn't the most comfortable wet-ball passer. Rich isn't, either. I don't know many quarterbacks who are, other than Brett Favre. So one of the things we incorporated into our practices with the Bucs is soaking the footballs, just the way I learned to do it back at Tennessee. You never know when you're going to get a violent thunderstorm in Tampa. If you don't practice a wet-ball exchange, how are you ever going to be ready for it in a game?

•

In the eyes of a lot of people, my relationship with Keyshawn Johnson is defined by his sideline tirade directed at me in front of the *Monday·Night Football* cameras during our September 23 game against St. Louis. That was one snapshot in a much larger photo album of our first season together, and it had absolutely nothing to do with how we got along before that moment or since.

Keyshawn wasn't the first player to get in my face. He won't be the last. What brought on that outburst in the Rams' game was that we decided to go with "U" personnel—two tight ends, two backs, one receiver. It's a good running formation because you can have a big tight end on both sides and balance the defense, and you can throw out of it if you choose to. I called, "U Keenan," which meant Keenan McCardell, who has caught 640 passes in his career, would be in on that particular play and Keyshawn had to come out. Keyshawn got mad and let me know about it on the sidelines. There really wasn't anything for me to say in response.

As a coach, my job is to keep looking at the big picture, keep striving to have the right group of players on the field for the right situation. That's why we have "U Keyshawn," where Keenan comes out and Keyshawn stays in. I'm sure Keenan isn't any happier about being on the sidelines than Keyshawn is. In our playoff game against San Francisco, we went with "U Jurevicius," when both "keys" to our success were on the sidelines, and we threw a touchdown to Joe Jurevicius.

You can't please everybody all the time. I just came from Oakland, where we had Jerry Rice and Tim Brown. We went with "U" personnel a lot there. I had to take Jerry Rice, the greatest receiver in the history of football, out of the game at times. He didn't like it, either. In Philadelphia, sometimes Irving Fryar came out of games. In Green Bay, it was Sterling Sharpe. Try dealing with that sort of thing with Sterling Sharpe and

Mark Clayton when you're a twenty-eight-year-old coach. . They're not going to yell at Mike Holmgren, so guess who they're yelling at?

On every sideline, I've seen players bitching at their coaches and vice versa. What world do you think we live in as NFL coaches? You've got fifty-three guys. Only forty-seven are active. They all want to play. There are going to be guys who get mad. Even the starters who aren't yanked out lose their temper if things aren't going the way they want them to.

It's like me playing in a scramble golf tournament. Every once in a while I get fired up, especially if our group is playing well. When the guy we're counting on to be our "A" player duffs a shot in a key situation, I'm going to yell, "What the hell are you doing?" It doesn't mean I don't love our "A" player.

It's like when you chastise one of your kids. When I yell, "Don't do that!" to one of my sons, it doesn't mean I don't love him. Yet when America sees the same sort of thing on TV, all of a sudden there's a "major rift" between the coach and the receiver. All of a sudden, the quarterback and the coach are "at odds." Give me a break.

# TWELVE

# Validation

## When It All Comes Together

There is nothing better than being able to share a Super Bowl victory
with a great player like Warren Sapp and everyone else connected
with the Buccaneers. (Tom Wagner/Tampa Bay Buccaneers)

I SENSED THAT OUR PLAYERS were uncomfortable before our season opener against New Orleans in Raymond James Stadium. They just didn't have any feel for what the new routine was going to be like with me as their coach. Do we pray before the game? Do we pray after the game? How is this coach, this "Chucky" guy, going to be if we lose? How is he going to be on game day? Are we allowed to have our music on in the locker room? Can we have the TV on to watch the other games before our game?

Even though we had gone through a four-game preseason, everybody was just a little bit tight. And it showed on the field. For the second time in my career, I lost a head coaching debut. The Saints beat us 26–20 in overtime when Tom Tupa, our punter and a former quarterback, tried a desperation throw from our end zone when he sensed that his kick in OT was going to be blocked. Tom is right-handed, so when Fred McAfee broke through and grabbed his right arm, Tom tried a left-handed pass. James Allen easily intercepted it in the end zone to give New Orleans the win. It wasn't quite as bad as that 28–8 loss at Kansas City in my first game with the Raiders, but we still didn't play worth a damn on either side of the ball.

I was especially disappointed that our defense had given up 368 yards. It seemed like the Saints had too easy a time moving up and down the field. So the night before our second game, in Baltimore, I wanted to get a clear message across to the defense. I called those guys out by calling out John Lynch because I knew he'd respond.

"John, I'm a great admirer of yours," I began. "I'm a great admirer of this defense. But we're 0–1. We're on the road. We need to win, okay?

"New Orleans comes to our town and gets four straight third-down conversions. What the hell are we doing, John? Can we address that this week? We've got a young quarterback we're facing in Chris Redman. He's had one career start. Do you have a little bit of a pissed-off feel about yourself tonight? Good. Take it out on Chris Redman and the Ravens tomorrow. Let's get our act together on defense.

"On offense, don't hallucinate when the ball is snapped. Play! Do we want to be a world-championship team? Do you guys want to dominate? Then dominate. Play like a champion, and don't worry about the consequences. Don't be afraid of success. Don't be afraid of being on the cover of every magazine in the world."

We wanted them to play football like they were capable of playing it. We needed that defense to help our offense by establishing good field position and creating turnovers. We needed those defensive guys to help us get our first win. As horrific as we played against the Saints, we were down 20–0 with about five minutes left, and Brad took us down on an impressive two-minute drive to make it 20–7. The defense got us the ball back again and our great kicker, Martin Gramatica, tied it at the end of regulation to force overtime. That told the defense to keep fighting, keep playing, keep working to get the ball back because the offense was going to do something with it.

In week two we shut out the Ravens 25–0. Even though we didn't score an offensive touchdown, we played very well offensively, holding the ball for more than thirty-five minutes. We had three great, long drives. We took the crowd out of it. We didn't have a turnover. Combine that with a dominant defensive performance, and that's a pretty unbeatable combination.

There wasn't a whole lot to say about our 20–10 loss in

Philadelphia on October 20. The Eagles beat us, ending our winning streak at five and extending the Buccaneers' Vet losing streak to three. But it wasn't as if we had played our best football. We gave up a long touchdown pass just before halftime. We had a season-low 207 yards of offense. Brad Johnson was sacked six times and had to leave the game with a rib injury in the fourth quarter. Yet with Rob Johnson at quarterback, we had a goal-line situation with four minutes left and we missed a short field goal.

Regardless of how poorly we played or our team's continued lack of success in Philly, it was too early to get discouraged. We didn't start getting into thoughts like *Gee, we lost our chance to have a bye in the playoffs. We lost our chance to have home-field advantage.* I just knew this: We weren't going to go anywhere if we didn't pick it up on offense. We had to play much better offensively just to get to the playoffs, let alone win in them. I was more concerned with getting our act together and winning the NFC South just for a chance to make the postseason than I was about anything else.

We did go on to win our next four games. Although we never really took off and became the most prolific scoring machine, we averaged almost twenty-seven points a game in Brad's last six starts of the regular season. Not coincidentally, our defense played great the rest of the season and wound up ranking first in the NFL. We won our division with a 12–4 record, best in franchise history. We were proud of that, but I knew that there was a lot more for us to accomplish.

The lone benefit to having the record we did is that it gives you a bye in the first round. For the players, it's a chance to rest and heal. As coaches, you try to take advantage of that extra time by projecting which team you're going to face in the next round and preparing accordingly.

The Packers were playing Atlanta at home in their wild-card

game. Naturally the Packers were the favorite because the Falcons were going from their nice, cozy dome to snowy and cold Lambeau Field, where the Packers had never lost a playoff game. At the same time, we knew the Falcons had the firepower to beat the Packers, because they should have beaten them at Lambeau in the season-opening game. We decided to play the percentages and started looking at a little Green Bay tape. Sure enough, Atlanta beat the Packers, meaning we would play San Francisco or the Giants, and those teams weren't going to face each other until the next day. After the Giants jumped out on top and looked like they were going to roll to victory, we started watching Giants tape. All of a sudden Jeff Garcia got hot and led San Francisco to a victory that came down to a botched field goal by the Giants, and we're starting all over again with 49ers tape. We never really got the advantage of a good extra night or night and a half of preparation.

We knew San Francisco had just been through an emotional, exhausting, come-from-behind 39–38 win over the Giants. Meanwhile, we were feeling fresh. Brad Johnson had missed the last two regular-season games with a right lower-back contusion. We needed the bye to get him well. We felt good about our plan.

We put together one of our most convincing games of the year to beat the 49ers 31–6. Being able to go back to Brad really gave our team a lot of juice. When the other players saw him taking snaps in pregame warm-ups in our stadium, they became very confident because they had seen how well the offense had performed during his last six starts. We scored touchdowns on three consecutive possessions to build a 28–6 halftime lead. Our defense played great that day as well, intercepting Garcia three times and forcing him to fumble once.

With the Eagles beating Atlanta the night before, we would have to go to Philadelphia for the NFC Championship Game. Right away, all you heard in the media were the reasons we had no chance of advancing to the Super Bowl. Three straight losses in Veterans Stadium. Two straight playoff losses there by a combined score of 52–12. No offensive touchdowns in three years. The Bucs' 0–9 record when the temperature dips below thirty degrees, which was supposed to be the case in this game.

On Wednesday I began our first big team meeting of the week by telling the players what they had been hearing from the moment the San Francisco game ended.

"They say we can't win in the Vet," I began. "We can't win in the Vet?"

I popped a tape into the video machine.

"That's Tampa Bay wearing orange jerseys and playing in Veterans Stadium," I said. "They've got this little rookie linebacker, number fifty-five. That looks like Derrick Brooks. They've got this big rookie defensive lineman, number ninety-nine. Isn't that Warren Sapp? They've got this third-year safety that seems out of position; he can't find the ball. I think that's John Lynch right there."

I showed about two or three plays, stopped the tape and said, "I was in my first year as the offensive coordinator of the Philadelphia Eagles in 1995, when this game was played. You came to Veterans Stadium and kicked our asses in the opening game. It was the most humiliating experience of my life. I'll never forget how horrible that feeling was—driving home at night with people yelling at me, flipping me the bird.

"Do you remember this game, Derrick? Warren? John? You guys have won in the Vet. We're only going to Philadelphia. It's in America. It's not like we're going out of the country."

After that we focused in on what we thought would be some of the keys to winning the game. As far as the coaching staff was concerned, the biggest was stopping Brian Mitchell, the Eagles' veteran kickoff-return man. We talked about that all week—morning, afternoon and evening. That was how big a factor we thought Brian Mitchell would be in determining the outcome. For whatever reason, we had not found a way to even contain this guy. He loved playing against us because he just always could count on breaking a big one, such as the forty-seven-yarder he had in October. After going through *NFL Films* footage of the Bucs' 2001 playoff game in Philadelphia, I found a clip of Mitchell, in slow motion, sprinting out from the tunnel with a look of excitement.

"He looks excited to see us, doesn't he?" I said. "He ought be; he owns us. WE'VE GOT TO STOP MITCHELL! There he is, number thirty. You've got to stop Mitchell!"

The day before the game, we were having our usual walk-through. It was quiet in the Vet. While the defense was going through its part of the session, I was talking with Keyshawn Johnson and Keenan McCardell.

"Hey, call me a name," I said to them.

"What?" Keyshawn said as he and Keenan looked at me like I was nuts.

"Call me a name."

"Jerk!"

"No, no. Give me your best stuff."

They started calling me foul names.

"Good, good," I said. "I'm just getting ready for tomorrow."

When I called, "Everybody up" at the end of the walk-through, I said, "Okay, Keyshawn. What am I?"

"You're a blond-headed, butt-bleeping bitch!"

"Got that, men? Because that's what you're going to hear tomorrow. That's all you're going to hear the whole game. You might as well get ready for it today."

At our team meeting that night, I set out to address the challenges we faced the next day, beginning with that 0–3 losing streak in the Vet. I told the players about being in Pac Bell Park in San Francisco one night to watch Barry Bonds, the home run king, against the Los Angeles Dodgers.

"I'm a big Dodger fan, and we make him look bad his first at-bat," I said. "He doesn't even get a good swing. Struck his ass out! Second time he comes up to bat, he doesn't get a real good swing then, either. Pops up to second. Next time up. Strike three looking, outside corner.

"Barry Bonds is 0 for 3 when he comes up in the eighth inning. Does anybody in here think Barry Bonds isn't going to swing away? Does anybody think Barry Bonds chokes up on his bat and takes pitches? Or does he stand in there and take his cuts?

"Barry Bonds stands in there, all right, and takes this little white baseball way out into the ocean for another home run. And that's what you've got to do. Take your cuts, man. Take your swing. Don't curl up thinking that you're going to strike out. Go in there and take your swings. Be Barry Bonds."

I used another baseball analogy to drive home the point that just because we were playing for the NFC title, in a place where we hadn't won in three years, there was no need for us to change our approach. I talked about how Randy Johnson, pitching on one day's rest, came in for the Arizona Diamondbacks in the ninth inning to get the Yankees out and win the World Series.

"Do you think Randy Johnson held his fastball any different?" I said. "Do you think Randy Johnson changed his delivery because he was throwing on one night's rest? Does anybody think that? No. He took the same windup, gripped the ball the same way and threw the same gas with the same location he always does. Perfect. And he got 'em out and he won the World Series."

In talking about the hostile Philly crowd and all the other distractions they could expect the next day, I switched to golf.

"Do you guys watch Tiger Woods play golf?" I asked the players. "I follow Tiger Woods. He walks from hole to hole, and on every hole he's got people giving him shit. They're tired of seeing him win. He's got good-looking girls distracting him, trying to get his phone number. You know what Tiger Woods does? He hits that ball straight down the middle, and all I ever see him do is pound his fist, pound his fist, shoot sixty-five and walk away with all the money, all the trophies. And he does it every tournament. That's what you've got to do tomorrow. Play *your* game. Be at *your* best. And don't worry about anything else.

"Offensively we haven't scored a touchdown here in three years. Three years. No touchdowns. HOW CAN WE DO WORSE? You got shutout. I got shutout. Why don't we go out and do something about it? DO SOMETHING ABOUT IT! Remember, you get what you deserve. Go get what you deserve tomorrow!"

What I had in mind by "get what you deserve" is that we would jump out to a fast start, take their crowd right out of it and just roar to a big win. I wasn't even picturing how the game actually began, with Brian Mitchell—the man we needed to stop to give us our best chance to win—returning the opening kickoff seventy yards and Duce Staley scoring two plays later on a twenty-yard run. I'm thinking, *Nice speech, Jon.*

That place is going berserk. They've got a 7–0 lead and there are still fourteen minutes go to in the first quarter of the NFC Championship Game. You just know what the fans and the Eagles are thinking: *We've got the Bucs beaten again. They haven't scored a touchdown here in three years. They aren't scoring one today.*

But we answer that score with a score of our own, a forty-eight-yard Martin Gramatica field goal. It isn't a touchdown, but it's huge because it lets everyone know that maybe this isn't going to be as easy as they think it's going to be.

We stop them on their next possession and on third-and-two we call, "Triple Left 83 Double Smash X Option." That's where we have two guys run corner routes, two guys in the flat, and Joe Jurevicius inside working off whoever is covering the hook route inside. The guy covering the hook varies depending on the defense they're in; in this case Barry Gardner, a linebacker, is one-on-one with Joe, who as a receiver should have the edge in that match-up. Joe makes a nice play to take it seventy-one yards.

The catch was huge. The fact that Joe was on the receiving end made it even bigger, because we didn't even know if he was going to play. Five days before the game, his wife, Meagan, gave birth two weeks prematurely and their baby, Michael, was extremely sick. When Joe came into my office to tell me he wasn't sure about his availability for practice or if he would even make it to Philadelphia, I told him to just go be with his wife and son—that there was nothing more important than his family. In a situation like that, all you can do is try to be as supportive as you can. I've got three little guys of my own, and I know a couple of people that have gone through what Joe and his wife were experiencing. It stops your life cold. It just puts everything into perspective. As I spoke with Joe, our game suddenly seemed kind of small.

He ended up missing three days of practice and he didn't get to Philly until the night before the game. But I wasn't at all worried about the lack of preparation posing a problem, because Joe's a very heads-up ballplayer. He met with his coaches and studied the plays and was up to speed with where to line up and what to run. He was able to handle it with ease. But there was nothing easy about what he and his wife were going through. Michael's illness was so severe that, sadly, he would pass away after the season. My heart goes out to Joe and Meagan. And I'll never forget Joe for showing unbelievable character and care for his teammates by playing in the game while his baby was still fighting for his life. I never heard Joe say this, but I think he played the game as much for his teammates as he played it for himself. I think that was a key motivator. He wanted to help his team win that game and he knew we needed him to do that.

After Joe's big catch, we've got a first-and-goal and we bring out "Y Hurricane" personnel. Warren Sapp, the former Miami Hurricane, jogs out there as an eligible tight end. He makes a big block at the point of attack on the left side and Mike Alstott scores our first offensive touchdown in Philadelphia in three years to give us a 10–7 lead at the end of the first quarter. I'm running down the sidelines yelling, "Should they stop the game and give you guys a Goddang game ball for scoring in the Vet? Is the commissioner here to make the presentation? That's probably all that we've got left offensively, right? We've got to be maxed out here for another five years, right?"

Our guys are loving it. The fans start booing. They can't believe the Eagles have given up an offensive touchdown to the Buccaneers. Before the day is over, they'll give up another touchdown by our offense, on a nine-yard pass from Brad Johnson to Keyshawn Johnson, as well as one by our defense, on a ninety-two-yard interception return by cornerback Ronde Barber.

It should be noted that, to help him grip the ball better, Brad wore a tacky glove for the first time in his career in that game. The glove had just started to make its way into football when I was the Eagles' offensive coordinator. With my small hands, grabbing a wet ball is a challenge, but when I tried on one of those gloves, I couldn't believe the difference. If only I could have had one when I was playing at Dayton. I never could convince any of the Eagle quarterbacks to wear one. Randall Cunningham certainly didn't need it with his huge hands. I did get Gannon to throw with one every now and then in practice, but he never wore one in a game when I was in Oakland because we never encountered any really wet weather. But in the final weekend of the 2002 season, I was watching the Raiders play the Chiefs in Oakland during a driving rainstorm. Sure enough, there was Rich with a glove on.

Brad had included that tacky glove in the little kit of extra gear that he carries with him to every game. Most players rely on the equipment staff to supply them with anything they might need beyond their basic uniform. Not Brad. He has his own little kit that has a change of jersey, a change of wristbands, a change of socks, a change of shoes. He keeps it with him at all times. Whereas a lot of guys wait until halftime to change any part of their uniform, Brad will change during a game, right on the sidelines. I'll say, "Brad, let's go; we've got the ball!" He'll be hurriedly changing his jersey or his socks, then go running onto the field. He just likes that fresh feel.

Brad went with the tacky glove that day because even though it wasn't raining or snowing, it was cold—twenty-six degrees at kickoff with a wind chill of sixteen. Throwing a brand-new ball that hasn't had all the slick factory coating rubbed off it is tough enough. Throwing a brand-new ball that's cold can be as difficult as throwing a wet ball. Brad went twenty for thirty-three for 259 yards and a touchdown in our 27–10 win. How much, if anything, did wearing the glove have to do with that? Who knows? All that mattered was that Brad felt good about having it on.

Our playoff journey was amazing in a lot of ways. For me, it felt like a trip down memory lane, like a fairytale.

We opened with the 49ers, the team that gave me my introduction to NFL coaching and employed my dad for sixteen seasons as a regional scout (I know he was rooting for us because blood is thick in our family). San Francisco was where I began to learn all about the "West Coast" offense. It was where George Seifert introduced me to the importance of organization and structure. It was where I got a firsthand look at the confident manner with which a coordinator, Mike Holmgren, is supposed to install an offense. It was where I saw the benefits of a coach, Ray Rhodes, speaking a language that players understand.

I had worked with Steve Mariucci, the 49ers' coach, in Green Bay, which was where I found out about the delicate nature of dealing with a strong personality like Sterling Sharpe. It was where I learned the value of having the courage of your convictions, as Ron Wolf and Mike did in making the bold and brilliant trade for Brett Favre, and learned how to get the very best from a free spirit, as Mike and Steve did from Brett. That ended up being Steve's final game with the 49ers. Now he's coaching the Detroit Lions. Three seasons after leading the Packers to a Super Bowl victory, Mike became executive vice president of football operations for the Seattle Seahawks. Ray is his defensive coordinator.

After our playoff victory over San Francisco, one of our security guys came into the coaches' room and said, "Bill Walsh would like to see you." I couldn't believe it. Bill, who is a consultant for the 49ers, just came down to say, "Congratulations on a great victory." That was a moment I'll never forget. It's almost as if you've come full circle. You run this gamut of emotions, from Dave Adolph coming into your office after you get your ass kicked by Kansas City, and five years later Bill Walsh is coming into your office congratulating you on beating his 49ers. Who'd have ever thought that would happen?

The next week we were playing in Philadelphia, where I spent three years as a coordinator. It was the last NFL game that would ever be played in Veterans Stadium, because the Eagles now call Lincoln Financial Field—a state-of-the-art facility where I seriously doubt you'll find any cats or rats—their new home. That was chilling to me. That was awesome. I had spent a lot of my life in Philadelphia. It was where I confronted the challenges of overseeing the whole offense rather than just one position. It was where I became involved with difficult decisions, such as benching Randall Cunningham, and discovered the need to adapt and adjust when you encounter the injuries like we did with Rodney Peete and Ty Detmer. It was where I had my first dealings with a player, Ricky Watters, that I simply never could connect with, even though his talent was vital to our success. It was where I received my first taste of high praise and harsh criticism from fans and media. It was where our second son, Michael, was born.

Andy Reid, the Eagles' coach, was also part of that staff we had in Green Bay, along with Dick Jauron, who now coaches the Chicago Bears. I had worked a lot of hours with Andy. If people call me a grinder, he's a double grinder.

I've known Jim Johnson, the Eagles' defensive coordinator, since I was nine years old, when he and my dad worked together at Indiana. Jim's son, Scott, whom I hadn't seen since we left the Cotton Bowl early in that ice storm, was at the NFC Championship Game with his mom and came down to the field beforehand to say hello.

You talk about the weird feeling of coming face-to-face with your past. I saw cornerbacks Troy Vincent and Bobby Taylor, safety Brian Dawkins, and running back Duce Staley—guys I had worked with and coached when I was in Philly.

It seemed to take forever for our chartered flight back to Tampa to even start to taxi, let alone take off. I don't know why, but I suspect maybe a few people who were part of that Philly ground crew were Eagle fans who just might not have been in too big of a hurry to see us depart on time—especially with the Super Bowl only a week away. It didn't really matter because it gave us that much more time to celebrate together as a team.

One of our PR guys updated me that Oakland had a pretty commanding lead over Tennessee late in the AFC Championship Game, so we had a pretty good idea that the Raiders would be our opponent in Super Bowl XXXVII. The pilot would make that official before we took off, but we really weren't thinking about the Super Bowl at that point. We just wanted to enjoy that win.

Obviously the whole angle of me going against the team I had coached in the four previous seasons and the crazy circumstances that landed me in Tampa were going to be big with the media. Some people went as far as to say that you couldn't have written a movie script any better than the way things turned out. I truly didn't care about that. To me, it was all about being in the Super Bowl. I felt so far removed from the Raiders, it was unbelievable. The one year in Tampa was so intense, Oakland felt like it was ten, twenty years ago. It really felt no different from playing against any of the other teams I had coached for. This was a big game. We had to have this game. It wasn't about going against my former team.

When we landed in Tampa, there must have been about forty thousand fans waiting for us. We had to set up a podium so that we could properly thank them for being there for us and hold up the NFC Championship Trophy. After fighting through all that traffic, we didn't get to bed until about three or four o'clock in the morning. I had to forget about the fact that I can function on almost no sleep most of the time and remember that there are people on our staff who do require a little bit of sleep. I wasn't going to ask them to lie in bed just for an hour or so and then meet me in the office.

I actually got about four hours of sleep, which was pretty good, considering the circumstances. Later that morning Rich McKay, our general manager, and I called Commissioner Paul Tagliabue to explain that our coaching staff had to remain in Tampa on Monday to work on our game plan. We hadn't gotten back from Philadelphia until the wee hours of Monday morning and we had about a five-hour flight ahead of us to San Diego. We proposed that we would send all our players and support staff out to San Diego on Monday, and then all the coaches would fly in at the crack of dawn on Tuesday to be part of Media Day at Qualcomm Stadium. The commissioner agreed. I wasn't trying to get an unfair advantage, but the Raiders had played at home and had only a forty-five-minute flight to San Diego.

We had a meeting with our players to tell them they were on their own. We appointed Simeon Rice, our killer defensive end, as team chaperone. He would be in charge of bed check Monday night.

"Carry the flag," I told the team. "Represent us well. And don't feel like you have to answer any questions from the media for me. You don't have to fight any of my battles. This is about you guys. It's about you against the Raiders. Enjoy this time because you've earned it. We'll see you guys when we get there."

The first thing we did as a staff was look at the tape of our game against Philadelphia to make sure we saw what the Raiders were looking at. What were we showing? What were we doing? What would they be preparing for?

From there we plunged right into our video cut-ups of the Raiders. I had coaches from our offensive staff briefing me on Oakland's base blitzes and nickel blitzes. My brother Jay, who had helped out on the offensive coaching staff the whole season, and Jeremy Bates, our offensive quality-control coach, synchronized the tapes just the way I like them. We worked until about ten-thirty, eleven o'clock that night.

About 4:30 A.M. Tuesday we boarded a chartered plane belonging to Dallas Mavericks owner Mark Cuban for our long trip to San Diego. Our owners, the Glazers, were able to reserve it for us, I'm sure at a considerable cost. I can't begin to say how huge they came through for us by doing that because it allowed all of us not only the chance to maintain somewhat of our same routine, but also to get a little bit of sleep before heading into twenty hours of game-plan preparation. It was an important asset. It's a classic example of owners providing their coaches with every possible resource to be successful. It just gives you that much more motivation to do everything in your power to come through for them.

During the flight, I got together with Monte Kiffin and gave him some notes about the Raiders' offense that I thought might

be helpful. We talked about some of the pass patterns I felt the
Raiders were going to run and some of the buzzwords and code
words they would use that might help him. I had a pretty good
idea about how their snap count was going to sound. I had
some inside information about Gannon and about the Raiders'
offensive system. I mean, I had been their head coach and I did
call a lot of their plays for four years. I realized they had
changed some of their playbook, but our defense had still seen a
lot of those offensive plays in our practices. Our snap count still
was similar to their snap count.

As soon as we landed, around 7 A.M. San Diego time, we had
a police escort take us to Media Day. I never saw anything like
that in my life—thousands of reporters and photographers from
all over the world jammed along one side of the stadium to
interview just about anyone wearing Buccaneer red, pewter,
black and orange. We were required to be there for an hour.
After that it was the Raiders' turn.

I knew what questions I was going to hear and I just set out
to answer them the best I could without giving the Raiders the
tiniest bit of material for added motivation (as if their guys or
our guys really needed one extra reason to be excited about
playing in the Super Bowl). My answers were probably boring,
but I was totally focused on the bull's-eye. I tried to stay oblivious to everything else that was going on. I got wind of some of
the critical comments that players I had coached in Oakland
made about me in the newspapers—how I had betrayed them
by leaving, how they were the victims, how I was a selfish guy
and all that stuff. But I let it go. Every time someone told me
something that somebody from the Raiders said about me, I
said, "I really don't care. I don't want to get involved in that.
It's not about me. It's about the Bucs and the Raiders. Super
Bowl XXXVII."

•

When we got to our hotel, our video equipment had all been set up, with all the tapes waiting for me. I continued studying the Raiders and—along with our coordinators, Bill Muir and Monte Kiffin, and special teams coach Rich Bisaccia—finalized the game plan late Tuesday night. The quality-control guys Xeroxed it, and we distributed it to the players Wednesday morning for practice that afternoon.

The whole experience was wild. I had never burned it at both ends before like I did that week. I ended up getting sick, really congested to the point where I could barely talk. I had watery eyes. I was fried. It was a long season, but those were the longest three days of preparation for a game that I had ever experienced. They were for a lot of our coaches. Nevertheless, I was confident about our plan. I was confident about how well we would play.

I told our players all week, "We're going to win this game."

We tried to maintain as much normalcy as we could with the players. We gave them Monday and Tuesday off, which is pretty close to the way our regular schedule runs before a Sunday game. We followed our usual practice routine, although there were a couple of little twists. I coached the scout team offense against our defense the whole week. That way I could make little important adjustments that I wanted our defensive guys to see, like certain shifts that I felt the Raiders might do. Sometimes I'd have the scout team offense hurry to the line quickly, when the defense would least expect it, and run a no-huddle attack. The idea was to make our guys play, make sure they were ready for all possibilities.

"These guys are going to throw the ball every play," I told the defense. "They barely ran the ball once against Tennessee. They think they can block you guys. They're going to send five guys out for passes. They're going to be throwing . . . every . . . single . . . play!"

The other twist came Thursday when I played quarterback in practice. Other than throwing some ball drills in San Francisco and Green Bay, it was the first time I had done that since my senior year at Dayton. I talked about it with Monte, and we decided that I would be under center for our final defensive period that day because it would provide the best simulation of what those guys could expect from an offense and a quarterback that I knew as well as anybody. I was nervous, man. The last thing in the world I wanted to do was look like a nonathlete in front of the players.

Just before I went in there, though, Monte called all the defensive players together and said, "Coach Gruden's going to play quarterback. He's going to let you guys get a little bit of a feel for Gannon—what he might do, how he might sound. He's not going to throw it, but he's going to give you a feel for the plays."

I'm thinking, *I'm not going to throw it? I never said I wasn't going to throw it.* When I got in the huddle I said, "Yeah, right, I'm not going to throw it. Okay, this is Bunch Left 300 Jet X Slant." I took the snap, I took a three-step drop and, boom, I threw a slant to Karl Williams for a gain. All of the offensive players and the backup defensive players watching let out a big "Whoa!" It was fun. I kept calling plays, using the exact same terminology I felt Gannon might use and calling signals in that same loud and clear style of his: "Red 88! Red 88!"

I wanted our defense to get that sense of Gannon on edge, attacking you every second. I made all kinds of hand signals the way Gannon does. I did a lot of pump fakes like he does because we knew that was how the Raiders generated a lot of their big plays; Rich does a great job of moving people out of position and finding vertical seams. I tried to be very confident, very much in charge. I even gave them the Rich Gannon staredown.

And the thing that really amazed me was that I was actually

throwing the ball pretty well. I couldn't believe it. I was making completions. I went no-huddle and we were moving so fast that I changed the play three times at the line because of the extra time we had on the play clock. Somehow I had become a damn good quarterback that day, and I don't care if you do think I sound arrogant when I say that. I was on fire. In a ten-minute stretch, I was Montana, Favre, Young, Brunell, Cunningham and George. I was amazing. At one point, I wondered, *Why the hell couldn't I ever play this way in college?*

As far as I was concerned, I had put together a hell of a sustained drive of about nine or ten plays. Of course, Simeon Rice told me afterward that he could have easily sacked me three times but held back out of sympathy because he saw I was having such a good time. I'm sure he did. And, yes, he probably would have made those sacks, too.

I don't know how much my playing quarterback helped in preparing our guys, but what it did more than anything was loosen them up. They had fun with it. They laughed their asses off. As I was walked off the field, I was tired. I think I pulled every muscle in my body, but I loved it. Probably the best compliment came from Brad Johnson. He had noticed that I called a "race" pattern, where the X receiver is supposed to run a square in. Our scout team receiver didn't run the right route and I threw the ball incomplete. It looked like I made a bad throw, but Brad knew what happened. "If the X had run the right route, it was open," he said. "That was impressive." I'll never forget that a Pro Bowl quarterback said something like that to me.

I knew we were ready to play on Thursday after we had the best nine-on-seven session that I'd ever been associated with. It was week twenty of our season, we had shoulder pads and shorts on, and it was crisp on both sides of the ball. It was just a lively, spirited, physical, well-executed portion of practice.

•

I didn't have any huge speech for the team the night before the Super Bowl. At that point there really isn't a whole lot to say. We were confident. We were prepared. We knew we were playing our best football. All I tried to do was keep everyone focused on the ultimate goal, which meant blocking out everything that could get in the way of it.

"Now you just beat Philadelphia," I said. "You're all excited, but that wasn't your Super Bowl. Tomorrow is your Super Bowl. The stadium is the same size as the one we play in. The dimensions of the field are exactly the same. The seating capacity is actually very much like Raymond James Stadium. There is going to be a little bit more pregame festivities than you're used to, so prepare for the long wait before they introduce the starting lineups, and there's going to be a longer halftime.

"But you're going to wake up tomorrow and you're going to play your best game ever. You're going to be world champions. World champions! Just do what you do."

I'll admit it felt a little weird during pregame warm-ups. When I was with the Raiders, I would always jog out and shake hands with Al Davis, who would be out on the field, watching the players warm up. He'd wish me good luck, I'd wish him good luck, and I'd say, "Let's get 'em, man." When I jogged out for pregame warm-ups before the Super Bowl, I looked over at the Raider players and I saw Al standing out there. I didn't know whether I should run over to him to shake his hand and say, "Good luck," or just avoid him. I decided avoiding him was the best way to go. I just didn't want to create any kind of a scene. That was probably the only weird part about the Super Bowl for me.

There were a lot of emotions running through me as I caught my first glimpse of Jerry Rice, Rich Gannon, Charlie Garner and Charles Woodson in seven-on-seven. As I've mentioned, I always look at the other team's players during pregame just to get an idea of how they look, how they're moving, any bit of information that might be helpful during the game. But that particular day, I kept my eyes off them. I just concentrated on our guys. I didn't want to peak emotionally too soon. I didn't want to become distracted. I was pretty focused on our game plan. I had a pretty good idea as to how we were going to approach them. Those Raider players know I respect them. Some of them know that I love them.

Just before we took the field for our warm-ups, Brad came up to me and said, "They've got seventy-five new balls for this game. There's no way they could have rubbed them all down. Do you think I ought to wear the glove?"

"It's up to you," I said.

At the start of warm-ups, he put the glove on and threw some passes. Then it took it off and threw more passes. Then he put it on again. When we got back to the locker room, Brad said, "Seventy-five new balls. I just don't think they can get to all of them."

"Hey, you're either wearing the glove or you're not," I said. "You're not wearing it for the first series and taking it off, because all that's going to do is create a distraction. Make up your mind. You're the man on this one."

I thought it was important for Brad to take charge of the situation and believe in whatever decision he made. It wasn't about the glove. It was about Brad's confidence. I honestly didn't think he was going to have too much of a problem in San Diego, where the temperature at kickoff was eighty-one degrees and the sky was clear. I should also point out that Brad has a sarcastic wit about him, and I still don't know to this day if he was being completely serious about his concern over the glove or if he was just messing with me in an effort to maybe loosen me up a little bit. Given that we were about to play the biggest game of our lives, I thought I should play it safe and take him seriously.

I don't predict the outcomes of any games, but I will say this:

If we're on our game, my God, anything can happen. When you have a seventy-seven-yard touchdown drive at the end of the half, like we did, and then come back with an eighty-nine-yard touchdown drive at the start of the third quarter, like we did, that's being on your game. And when you play the kind of defense we played, limiting them to sixty-two yards in the first half and intercepting a great quarterback like Rich Gannon five times and returning three of those interceptions for touchdowns, you're on your game.

Brad finally decided not to wear the glove. He went eighteen for thirty-four for 215 yards and two touchdowns in our 48–21 victory. God love Brad. God love all our players.

People want to give me credit for that defensive performance, for putting our guys in a situation where they could anticipate just about everything Rich and the rest that offense was going to do. But the fact is, opposing quarterbacks had a passer rating of forty-four-something against our defense in 2002. It didn't matter what kind of passing offense these guys saw. They got interceptions, they got sacks, they got turnovers, they got touchdowns against everybody. Under the able direction of Monte Kiffin and Rod Marinelli, they defended the pass better than any team in the league. The Super Bowl was no exception.

As soon as the game was over, almost like magic, confetti was flying all over the place and we were up on a platform in the middle of the field, waiting for Commissioner Tagliabue to present us with the Vince Lombardi Trophy. One of my favorite songs is "It's My Life," by Jon Bon Jovi. It basically says what I have always believed—that you've got to live your life while you're here, that you've got to get the most out of every day and every minute. As we're standing on that platform, guess who is on another platform that night? Jon Bon Jovi. He's singing my fight song.

Is that weird or what?

•

Winning a Super Bowl doesn't make me love football any more than I did the first time I pulled on my Leroy Kelly jersey and that plastic orange Browns helmet. Now, did I feel any better after we won the Super Bowl than I felt after we beat Philadelphia in the NFC Championship Game or after we stunned Kansas City with a come-from-behind win at Arrowhead when I was with the Raiders or after we beat Murray State when I was at Southeast Missouri? Yeah, I probably did, because it was for the world championship. It's a signature game. It's in the record books.

Somebody told me that, at thirty-nine, I'm the youngest coach ever to win a Super Bowl. That's really not accurate. When you talk about sleep deprivation—when you factor in the alert, nonsleep hours that I've had my whole life—I'm actually one of the older coaches in football history. At least that's what I've heard from many sleep-deprivation experts.

But I can honestly say that nothing about my approach to this job has changed or will change as a result of what took place on January 26, 2003. If you were at any of our practices this offseason or during training camp, you'd have seen the same guy you saw coaching quarterbacks in Cape Girardeau, Missouri, and receivers in Green Bay. I can't begin to tell you how proud I was of our red-zone execution on May 4, 2003. That was the last day of our minicamp. We were eighteen for twenty-one against the number-one-ranked defense in the NFL, and I was so fired up. Honest to God, I was very, very excited about it.

What winning the Super Bowl does provide is validation that all that time I missed with my wife and my kids was worthwhile. At least we have a world championship to show for it. Maybe now it's a little easier to understand why I get up so early, why I come home so late, why we always work on Fridays. There's also nothing better than sharing an accomplishment of that magnitude with so many other people—with

Monte Kiffin and Rod Marinelli, with Brad Johnson and Keyshawn Johnson, with Warren Sapp and Derrick Brooks, with everybody else on the team and in our organization, with my wife and boys, with my mom and dad, with my brothers.

And it was very special to share it with the Glazers, who went to great measures to give me this opportunity. I am forever grateful to them for that. I really enjoyed sitting with Joel and Bryan Glazer, as well as Mr. Malcolm Glazer and his wife, Linda, on the plane ride home and watching a replay of the Super Bowl on the TV monitors. You know you can never live up to that kind of compensation. Hell, who can? I certainly wasn't holding up my end when I was getting my ass kicked in my first game as an offensive coordinator in Philadelphia or when Kansas City thumped me in my Oakland debut or when New Orleans gashed me in my Tampa debut. You've got to get over games like that and show the resiliency to come back. And when you win your first division championship as a head coach and then win another one and then win a Super Bowl, you've got to get over those games, too. You can't sit there and rub your ring and read your scrapbook forever.

Fortunately, I know what a humbling business this is. The previous two teams that got to the Super Bowl didn't even make the playoffs the next year, so you'd better not get too fat and happy. You have to remember that the football gods are always watching. George Hallas is sitting up there. He's with Vince Lombardi and George Allen and Bobb McKittrick and Walter Payton, and they're watching. They're waiting for the Super Bowl champions to go to another banquet, to go have another steak dinner and another big piece of cherry pie. They want you to just fatten up like a big red tomato so that they can take a big bite out of you. Those are guys who love football and hate anyone who disrespects the game.

How do you disrespect it? By thinking you're a genius. By thinking you're really a smart guy. By starting to delegate more.

By coming to work a little bit later. Don't do your offseason research. Don't hold your players to any kind of standards. Let's cut back on the time they spend in the weight room and on conditioning. Let's take an extra day off. Let's just go fishing and have some fun.

This is a hard game. Not everyone can play it. Even fewer can play it well enough to win a championship. But when you do win one, maybe you gain even more confidence from it than you had before. Maybe your whole team does. A year ago we didn't have a single person at One Buc Place who had ever had a Super Bowl ring. Not one coach. Not one player. Not one person in our front office. Now we've got a bunch of them.

The people I've met who have made great accomplishments in different walks of life don't stop after the first one. You don't stop competing. You don't stop hungering for a championship. If anything, you take more responsibility to come back and win another one.

For anyone who doubts that, particularly anyone who plays for the Tampa Bay Buccaneers, I have only one question: "Do you love football?"

# ACKNOWLEDGMENTS

To TELL THE STORY about a career that has been helped by so many different people along the way, we reached out—and received—even more help. We want these individuals to know how much we appreciate their time, effort, support and caring. We couldn't have done it without you.

The very first person we wish to acknowledge is Cathy Hemming of HarperCollins. There is no question that you love football, Cathy, and that made for an ideal partnership from the start.

We can't thank Mauro DiPreta enough for his deft editing, wisdom, counsel and tremendous patience. As literary coaches go, you're one of the very best.

Thanks, too, to Joelle Yudin for her able assistance in handling the detail work at HarperCollins. We offer similar recognition to Mark Arteaga, who is as fine an administrative assistant as any coach could have.

We are thankful to Bob and Lynn LaMonte for their role in getting this project off the ground and for always being there to lend a hand. Basil Kane continues to set the standard for literary agents with his professionalism and integrity, and we are grateful for all that you did to make this book a reality.

In addition, we would like to express our gratitude to Jim

and Kathy Gruden, Cindy Gruden, Monte Kiffin, Jeff Kamis, Zack Bolno, Tom Wagner, Derek Boyko, Ed Mahan, Jeff Blumb, Chris Callies, Armen Keteyian, Doug Hauschild, Ron Hines, Justin Maskus, Rhonda Carucci and Chris Glenn.

      —*Jon Gruden,*
       TAMPA, FLORIDA
      —*Vic Carucci,*
       EAST AMHERST, NEW YORK